Getting to No.1 on Google

Harlow, England • London • New York • Boston • San Francisco • Toronto • Sydney • Auckland • Singapore • Hong Kong
Tokyo • Seoul • Taipei • New Delhi • Cape Town • São Paulo • Mexico City • Madrid • Amsterdam • Munich • Paris • Milan

PEARSON EDUCATION LIMITED

Edinburgh Gate
Harlow CM20 2JE
United Kingdom
Tel: +44 (0)1279 623623
Fax: +44 (0)1279 431059
Web: www.pearson.com/uk

First published 2013 (print)

ISBN: 978-0-273-77477-8 (print)

British Library Cataloguing-in-Publication Data
A catalogue record for the print edition is available from the British Library

Library of Congress Cataloging-in-Publication Data
A catalog record for the print edition is available from the Library of Congress

10 9 8 7 6 5 4 3 2 1
17 16 15 14 13

Print edition typeset in 11/14pt ITC Stone Sans Std by 3
Printed and bound in Great Britain by Scotprint, Haddington, East Lothian

NOTE THAT ANY PAGE CROSS REFERENCES REFER TO THE PRINT EDITION

Getting to No.1 on Google

in Simple steps

David Amerland

Use your computer with confidence

Get to grips with practical computing tasks with minimal time, fuss and bother.

In *Simple Steps guides* guarantee immediate results. They tell you everything you need to know on a specific application; from the most essential tasks to master, to every activity you'll want to accomplish, through to solving the most common problems you'll encounter.

Helpful features

To build your confidence and help you to get the most out of your computer, practical hints, tips and shortcuts feature on every page:

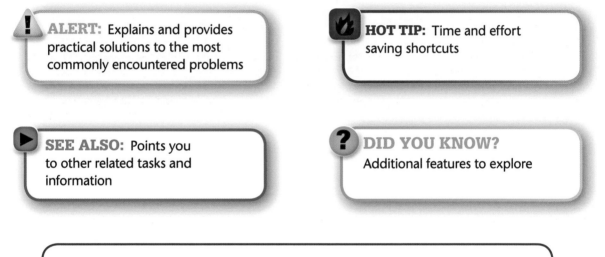

ALERT: Explains and provides practical solutions to the most commonly encountered problems

HOT TIP: Time and effort saving shortcuts

SEE ALSO: Points you to other related tasks and information

DID YOU KNOW? Additional features to explore

WHAT DOES THIS MEAN? Jargon and technical terms explained in plain English

Practical. Simple. Fast.

in Simple steps

About the author:

David Amerland is a British journalist. He has been actively involved in the Web and search since 1995 when the Internet became a viable means of online commerce. A former journalist, he has worked in the retail and business communication sectors for, among others, the John Lewis Partnership. He has transferred his experience of what works in the offline world to help create brands and visibility into his work online. Currently he is involved in guiding international companies in how to create successful SEO and social media marketing campaigns. He has taught courses on the subject for Rutgers University in New Jersey and he is present frequently, as a speaker, at industry conventions.

Dedication:

To N, as always.

Acknowledgements:

No book is every written in a vacuum and this is no exception. Special thanks need to go to Meg Tufano, Leland LeCuyer, Susanne Ramharter and Robert E. del Sol for permission to include them in the 'conversation' of this book and endless, thought-provoking discussions. In writing this I would like to thank my partner for putting up with my long hours, Nike, for telling me when enough was enough and I had to come away from my laptop screen, and Neil Salkind for being the kind of agent every writer should have. Last but not least, a special thanks should go to Viv Church for keeping me a more honest writer than I might otherwise have been.

Publisher's acknowledgements:

Photos: on p. 122, Hugh Hefner image courtesy of Getty Images; wedding images courtesy of Diamond Event Planners.

Screenshots: all Google and Google+ screenshots courtesy of Google, Inc.; pp.9 and 115 courtesy of Disqus; pp. 10, 12, 90, 133, 139, 155, 162, 164 courtesy of Twitter, Inc.; pp.10, 12, 89, 133, 155 courtesy of Facebook, Inc.; p.34 courtesy of Hyperspin; pp.43 and 44 courtesy of SemRush; pp.45 and 46 courtesy of Open Site Explorer; p.92 courtesy of Portent Interactive; p.107 courtesy of HubSpot; pp.116 and 117 courtesy of Livefyre; p.122 reprinted with permission from Yahoo! Inc. 2012 Yahoo! Inc. YAHOO! and the YAHOO! logo are trademarks of Yahoo! Inc.; pp. 136 and 137 courtesy of TweetReach, p.138 courtesy of Circle Count; p.157 courtesy of Bottlenose.

In some instances we have been unable to trace the owners of copyright material, and we would appreciate any information that would enable us to do so.

in Simple
steps

Contents at a glance

Contents

5 SEO strategies and your business

6 Analysing SEO performance

10 The real-time Web and SEO

Top 10 Google Problems Solved

Top 10 Google Tips

Tip 1: Create a Google Account

A Google Account is required to help authenticate your website, which then becomes a ranking factor in Google's search.

1 To create a Google Account go to https://accounts.google.com/, click Sign Up and simply fill in the details in the right-hand box.

2 Add as much information as possible. Make sure that you use your real name (this is important) and provide a means of additional contact (telephone or alternative email).

3 Click Submit.

HOT TIP: The more information you put in the fields when you fill in your Google account, the more functionality you are going to enjoy.

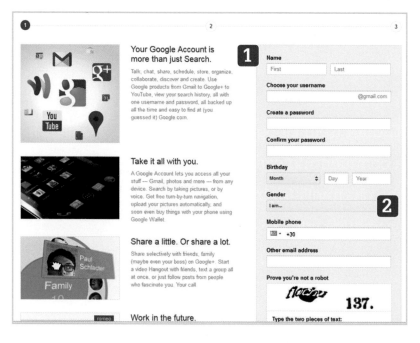

? DID YOU KNOW?

A Google Account is Google's means of providing a 'key' which unlocks all of its services. From Gmail to Google Plus, YouTube and Google Search, you will experience a much deeper integration if you have a Google Account.

HOT TIP: Google is creating an online identity service. Your Google Account becomes part of your online activity and the more Google is convinced that you are a real person, the higher the trust factor it places on what you do.

Tip 2: Optimise your website using online tools

There are free online tools from Google which will help you optimise your website and improve performance. To take advantage of them you will need to use your Google Account.

1 Go to https://developers.google.com/pagespeed/ and press Analyze. It takes a minute or two and then the results will be displayed below.

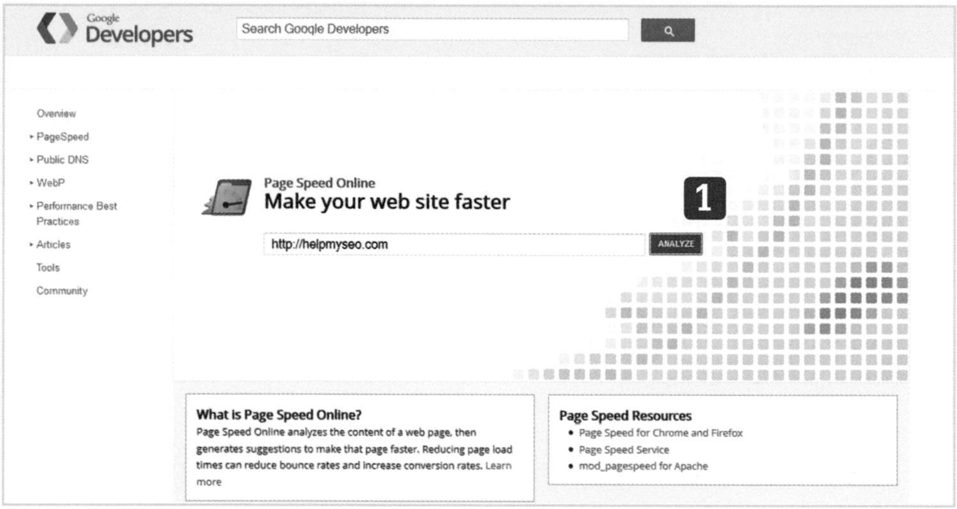

? DID YOU KNOW?

Search technology changes on a monthly basis, which means that a website that was perfectly well optimised at the beginning of the year may not be so well optimised by the middle of that year. Make a point of checking your website using this tool on a monthly basis.

! ALERT: You can use Google's website optimiser without logging into your Google Account. However, by logging in you enable the sharing of data which helps Google create better SEO tools, like this one.

2 Google's optimising tool will deliver its verdict in a website score out of 100 and colour-coded tasks.

a High priority – to be seen to as soon as possible.

b Medium priority – that may take more work to implement.

c Low priority – which should be last on your list.

d Experimental rules – which usually means optional.

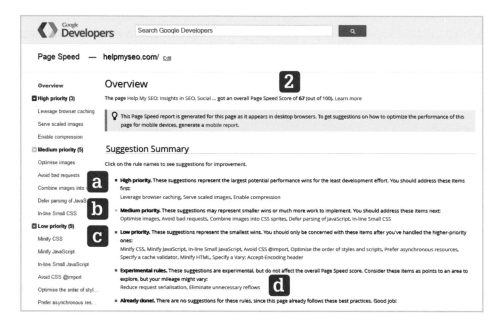

Tip 3: Research keywords for content

There are several ways to research the best keywords. It's best to log into your Google Account from the outset here. Once you've done that, go to http://goo.gl/8AkZU.

? **DID YOU KNOW?**

Local search volumes (the number of people searching for a particular query) and global search volumes for particular search queries are different. The information allows you to more precisely target online visitors to your site.

1 Input your search term.

2 Add your website.

3 Choose the best category.

4 Tick Only show ideas closely related to my search term.

5 Choose region and language for greater localisation.

🔥 **HOT TIP:** Google is far from impartial when suggesting terms. Make sure that you keep your keyword groups as tightly clustered as possible by always ticking the Only show ideas closely related to my search term box in the Google Keyword Suggestion tool.

Tip 4: Use Webmaster Tools for higher ranking

The Search queries section of Google Webmaster Tools can provide you with the vital clues and information you need to help improve your website's ranking.

1 Number of queries your site was served for.

2 The number of impressions resulting from the queries.

3 The number of clicks delivered.

4 The search queries that were used.

5 The number of impressions for each query.

6 The average ranking of your site for that query.

Query	Impressions	Clicks	CTR	Avg. position
froogle	12,000	16	0%	8.1
google places login	6,500	<10	-	11
"powered by fox contact" s	3,000	<10	-	340
blackhat seo google penalty	2,500	<10	-	9.4
"powered by fox contact" w	2,000	<10	-	230
"powered by fox contact" n	2,000	<10	-	280
seo help	1,600	<10	-	13

HOT TIP: Google Webmaster Tools now delivers more accurate website ranking for specific keywords than before.

? DID YOU KNOW?
Many of the keywords which deliver traffic to your website no longer appear in Google Analytics. Webmaster Tools has become necessary to plug the gap.

Tip 5: Set up Google Alerts

You need to monitor your website if you are to have an idea where your content appears. Google allows you to set up a monitoring search which will automatically keep track of the mentions of your website across the entire Web. For this you will need your Google Account login and password.

1 Go to www.google.com/alerts.

2 Fill in the search query field with the term you want to look for.

3 Use the drop-down boxes to refine what you want to look for.

4 Look at some of the results which Google finds for you.

5 Press Create Alert.

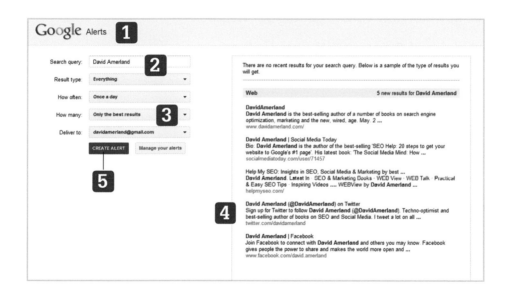

? DID YOU KNOW?
You can create up to 1,000 alerts and Google will deliver a summary of the results straight to your inbox.

🔥 HOT TIP: When you set up your alerts do not limit yourself to your website name. Set up alerts which use search terms in your industry and keep tabs of what your competitors are doing.

Tip 6: Mine SEO data from Google

Google Analytics is a powerful SEO tool which draws data directly from Google's Index. If the code is not already on your website you can see how to set it up here: http://goo.gl/EqHTW.

Go to your Google Analytics account and log in. Your dashboard gives you the following:

1 Number of daily visits.

2 Average time a visitor spends on your site.

3 Goal conversion rate (if you have set up Goals).

4 A break-down of how visitors get to your website.

5 A break-down of the country they come from.

🔥 HOT TIP: Goals set up on your website allow you to assign a monetary value to each visitor who reaches that stage and therefore track the worth of your traffic in sterling figures.

Tip 7: Choose a commenting system for your website

There are several commenting systems you can use. Some are native to website programming and others need to be installed. The latter have a distinct advantage over the former as they allow you to tap into their own already created communities and give you the possibility of attracting even more traffic that way.

- Specific login allows you to create a profile and become a member of the existing community.
- Log in using any existing social network login.
- Disqus community members can see comments and topics themselves and get to your website.

DID YOU KNOW?
Commenting systems offer several different ways of controlling spam and moderating comments, placing you in total control of what is added to your website.

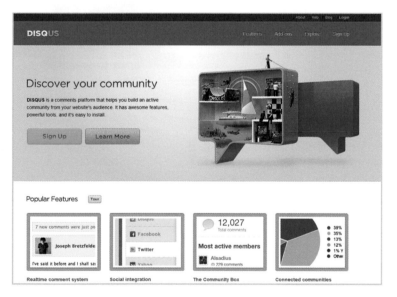

HOT TIP: A commenting system acts like an interlinked messaging system within the commenting system community. This has the power to start off and enhance conversations between commenting system community members, which take place right on your website.

Tip 8: Choose the channels for marketing your website

Social media marketing is time intensive. Its requirement that you devote at least some time in generating interaction and responding to it presents a challenge many businesses struggle to overcome. Your choice of network is important.

1 Google Plus is a social network which helps you connect with potential customers across the globe.

2 Twitter allows you to make use of the real-time web to connect with potential customers on time-sensitive issues.

3 Facebook connects you to friends and contacts from the real world.

ALERT: Post content from your website to social networks but only after the additional, explanatory text and its tone have been carefully worked out as it creates the context of your social network contact and helps create your online persona.

? DID YOU KNOW?
Research statistics show that Twitter is the best social platform possible for developing a brand and increasing brand recognition.

HOT TIP: Save time by linking up your Facebook account to Twitter by following the instructions on http://goo.gl/NqGke. The 140-character limit of Twitter is more forgiving than any of the other social networks, which require a lot more time and attention.

Tip 9: Learn to socialise your SEO

Use the power of social media to help your SEO further by leveraging your contacts and immediate online network of friends to boost your website content.

1 Use your Google Profile to log on to Google Plus.

2 Share your content in the public stream.

3 Use the Ripples tracking option to see the interaction in terms of re-shares to see how many it has reached.

HOT TIP: Increase interaction, comments and re-sharing by posting content which is interesting from an informational point of view and answers a crucial question your online audience may have, or by posting content that is fun to read.

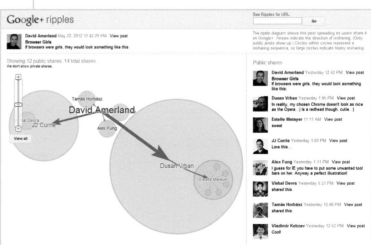

ALERT: Content that is fact-heavy in an overly assertive way discourages interaction and comments as those who read it feel that they are not expert enough to interact with it.

? DID YOU KNOW?

Content that is interacted with and re-shared in the Google Plus network generates a social signal which Google uses to assess its importance in the search index. This directly affects your website's ranking.

Tip 10: Establish a real-time Web presence

There is only one real-time Web channel and that is Twitter. Facebook has recently changed its stream to be closer to Twitter's immediacy in terms of its refresh rate. There is a distinct SEO advantage in having a presence in both networks.

1 Have a Twitter profile which reflects your business or brand.

2 Populate your Twitter stream by following some people in your industry.

3 Tweet often about your specific topics.

> **? DID YOU KNOW?**
> Use Twitter to market time-sensitive content. The links included in Twitter's 140-character message are indexed by Google and become part of your website's social signal.

> **⚠ ALERT:** Use Twitter frequently throughout the day to reach as many of your followers as possible. Studies show that you can only hope to reach a maximum of 7–10% of your followers on a single Tweet so it is important to Tweet often.

> **🔥 HOT TIP:** Twitter allows you to link it up to your Facebook profile and kill two birds with one stone by having your Tweets appear in your Facebook Timeline. This amplifies the reach of your Twitter marketing and social signal and helps your website's ranking in the SERPs.

1 Search engines and your business

Introduction

Search engines have become critical. As the Web has grown to an incredible number of websites, search has become the means through which web surfers find what they are looking for and websites are found. If you want your business to attract extra customers on the Web, you need to be on Google's first page for those search terms which reflect what you do. While this is simple to say, it is far from simple to achieve. Search engine optimisation (SEO) is not about making websites rank higher than they should. It is, instead, about helping website owners understand what they need to do in order to help search engines rank their websites properly.

In this chapter you will learn the basics of ranking on search. You will find out why some sites rank above others on Google's top pages and how you can take the steps necessary to outrank them. You will learn to assess your website from a search engine perspective and to use tools which will help you manage your SEO needs, yourself.

Understand ranking factors

There are only ten places on Google's first page for a result to appear in response to a search term a user has entered in the Google search box. Statistics compiled by digital analytics company ComScore show that 94% of those who conduct a search click on one of the results on Google's first page, which means that only 6% go to the second page and beyond. This staggering fact highlights the importance of a first-page Google ranking for your website.

- To illustrate how ranking works we will do a Google search for the term 'SEO help for my website', which is a cry for help many a business owner has to make at some point or another.

- The term is extremely competitive, with more than 75 million competing pages in the Google Index.

- My website appears in position #7 for that search term, on Google's #1 page. It becomes even more amazing if I tell you that the last time I optimised my website for that search term was 2010. In all this time it has been on the first page of Google.

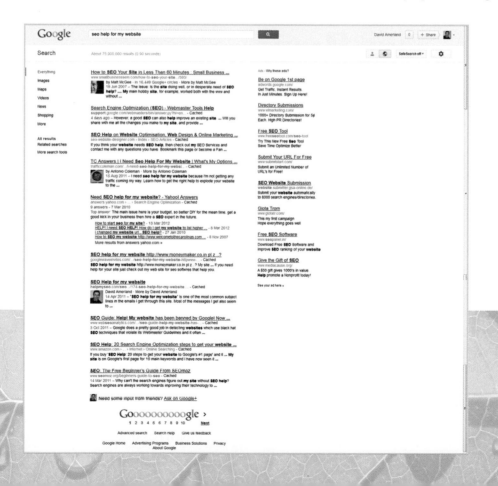

Individually none of the steps here would get the website to Google's #1 page against websites which have been actively working for that search term all this time. Together, however, they have proved to be a winning combination which has withstood the test of time and has kept my website on Google's first page for that search term for well over two years.

1 The search term 'SEO help for my website' is one which many business owners and webmasters search for. We can find out information like this easily (we will see how this is done a little later in the chapter).

2 In this case Helpmyseo.com has content which matches the search term exactly.

3 The website is linked to a Google Account to my website, giving it an extra level of authority.

4 The URL of this page of content is: http://helpmyseo.com/seo-blog/174-**seo-help-for-my-website**.html. You can see from the part of the URL in bold that it matches the search term exactly.

5 Clinching it, the search term is included in the opening line of the post.

? DID YOU KNOW?
Because it's so important to have the right results on Google's first page, Google search engineers carry out over 40 different adjustments to Google's search algorithm each month. That's more than 500 changes a year!

HOT TIP: Despite the high number of pages which compete against yours, you can get your website to the first page of Google if you have web pages which contain unique information, which has true value for the end-user.

Create a Google Account

Until 2011 the only reason you might have needed a Google Account was because you used the free email service, Gmail. In June 2011 Google introduced its own social network, called Google Plus, and changed everything in the world of SEO. Now a Google Account is required to help authenticate your website, which then becomes a ranking factor in Google's Search. Here you will create a Google Account.

1 Go to https://accounts.google.com/, click Sign Up and fill in the details in the box on the right-hand side.

2 Add as much information as possible. Make sure that you use your real name (this is important) and provide a means of additional contact (telephone or alternative email).

3 Click Submit.

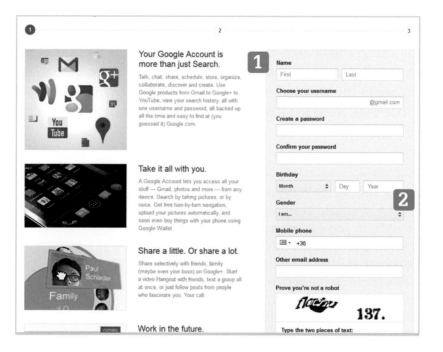

? DID YOU KNOW?

A Google Account is Google's means of providing a 'key' which unlocks all of its services. From Gmail to Google Plus, YouTube and Google Search, you will experience a much deeper integration if you have a Google Account.

HOT TIP: Google is creating an online identity service. Your Google Account becomes part of your online activity and the more Google is convinced that you are a real person, the higher the trust factor it places on what you do.

Assess your own website

To optimise your website, you need to know where it stands currently. It helps to see it with the eyes of a search engine because you will begin to understand what search engines look at. This will also allow you to understand why the structure of your website is important and whether there are any parts of it which are blocked to a search engine.

1 In order to assess your website go to www.webconfs.com/search-engine-spider-simulator.php.

2 Type in your website's URL address in the field box and press Enter.

- *What human visitors to your website see.* They can see the design and programming which make the site look attractive and then the navigation and content, including any pictures, flash elements and perhaps even video. Navigation buttons take them to other parts of the website.

- *What the search engine sees.* Google's bot sees a whole lot of text together and a bunch of links leading to other pages. If you do not see the same number of links you see in the visual display of your site reflected in the text display that the Google bot sees, it means that your site design is stopping your site from being indexed properly.

ALERT: Your ranking will suffer if you do not have adequate description on the photographs you use on your website. It will also suffer if you use excessive amounts of programming which are invisible to search engines. Remember, search engine bots cannot see pictures, video, javascript and flash programming.

WHAT DOES THIS MEAN?

Bots (or spiders): These are the pieces of programming search engines send out to crawl websites, grab the information and bring it back to be indexed. If your website is not easy to read to a bot then not all of its information will be indexed and you will miss out on valuable traffic.

Understand how search volume affects your business

The success of your business depends entirely on your ability to research those search terms related to your industry which deliver reasonable traffic and then optimise your website for them accordingly. Researching search terms is easy to do. The tools you need are available free online and we will examine them here.

The starting point for your research in online traffic for specific search terms which relate to your business is Google's Insights for Search, a free online tool: www.google.com/insights/search/.

1 Decide what the main search term is for the business you are in (e.g. lace-up trainers, black basketball shoes, barefoot running shoes, etc.). Input that in the first field box.

HOT TIP: Every visitor who comes to your website through search helps you. The number of visitors to your website is a search ranking metric used by Google to assess your website's SEO status.

2 If you have additional search terms you want to research click on Add search term. A new field box will appear which will enable you to input the next search term. You can repeat the process, adding as many as five different search terms here.

3 Decide how you are going to drill down to all this data. Is what you are researching likely to be found in web search, image search or news search? Is the data you are looking for global (will you be trading globally) or local? Pick the relevant time period and decide on the best category.

4 Press Search and get instant results.

Use Google Webmaster Tools

You need a Google Account to use Google Webmaster Tools. Google Webmaster Tools require a little technical know-how as you will need to prove you are the owner of the website you are checking. You will be given step-by-step instructions on how to do this and there are several methods.

With Google Webmaster Tools you can do the following:

1 Check your website's configuration to make sure that everything is exactly as it should be and there are no crawl errors (important for proper indexing).

2 Find search queries and see what brings people to your site.

3 See how the search queries match up against what you think brings people to your site.

> **SEE ALSO:** Create a Google Account earlier in this chapter.

4 See impressions, which are the number of times pages of your website have appeared on Google Search over a given time.

5 See clicks, which are the number of clicks which brought online visitors from Google Search to your website.

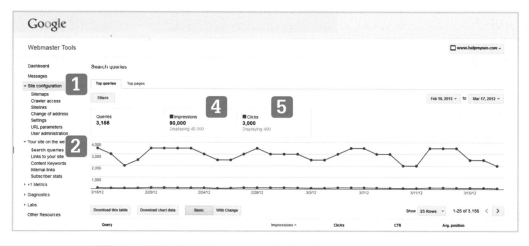

WHAT DOES THIS MEAN?

Google Analytics: This is another must-have free tool you need to install on your website. Google Analytics (www.google.com/analytics/) tells you how your website performs on Google Search.

HOT TIP: Google Analytics has a handy real-time traffic-monitoring option which allows you to see, in real time, the number of visitors who come to your site and the geographic region they come from.

Know what website ranking elements you control

Knowing which ranking elements you control and which you do not allows you to make better decisions on where you should focus your time and energy. Should you ever decide to outsource part of your online marketing it is important to know what you are paying for, and how to assess it.

1 Menu items which appear on your website.

2 Titles and headlines which appear on your website.

3 The frequency with which you create content on your website.

🔥 **HOT TIP:** Menu items lead to deeper indexing and their names become part of your website's analysis on the Google Index which determines how your website will be grouped in Google search.

❓ **DID YOU KNOW?** Titles and headlines frequently become a website ranking signal, so choose them with care.

❓ **DID YOU KNOW?** Frequency determines quite a few things, like how often Google will crawl your website and how 'fresh' your website's content will be. Content, in turn, will be determined by your own ability to write, the inclination to do so and the type of business you are in.

⚠️ **ALERT:** Google does not treat all websites equally. The Google bot arranges to visit your website depending on how often Google thinks you update your website's content. Also, depending on how original your website's content is, Google will group your site in the category of sites it values more or less. In the former you get to rank higher for specific search queries while in the latter you do not.

Learn how to see Google rankings

In order to track the progress of your optimisation efforts and know exactly what you need to pay attention to on your website in terms of specific content and keywords you need a way to assess the ranking of your website in Google Search.

To check your rankings go to www.seocentro.com/tools/search-engines/keyword-position.html.

1 Put in the search term you want to check. It can be one of your main keywords, a search phrase relevant to your business which you are optimising your site for, or a two-word combination.

2 Type in your domain name using either www.mydomainname.co.uk or http://mydomainname.co.uk where 'mydomainname' is replaced by your site name and then press 'Submit'.

3 You will be able to see your rank in the first 50 results on Google, Yahoo! and BING expressed as a number out of 50. This indicates your site's position in those search engines for that particular search term.

HOT TIP: You should check frequently on the keywords your site ranks for and the number of competing web pages. It helps give you an idea of how your website rankings are faring.

DID YOU KNOW?

Google rankings change every day in response to a number of factors. There is never any guarantee that your search rankings will remain steady. This is why you need to check regularly so that you have a clear idea of how your website is doing.

Understand the factors which affect your website's ranking

For some time now Google has deployed refinements in its algorithm which allow it to personalise search results and present locality-sensitive data to those who use its search. To help businesses take advantage of local traffic, much of which now is driven by the use of mobile devices such as smartphones and tablets, Google has created a free service called Google Places.

Go to www.google.com/places. You will need your Google Account login and password you registered at the beginning of this chapter.

1 Fill in all your business details, including phone numbers.

2 Put your physical address in Google Maps. This will benefit your business in terms of local search on mobile devices and it will also make it possible to find your business on Google's universal search when it serves localised results to those looking for your products or services.

HOT TIP: The contact details you input in Google Places are visible on mobile device search and will enable those who find your business to call you, directly.

HOT TIP: Google is incredibly good at indexing information and serving it up locally. Street addresses in your contact details, local phone numbers and postcodes, as well as any landmarks, are all useful when it comes to helping your website appear on search results powered by locality.

3 Fill in the rest of the form, putting in as many details as possible regarding how you can be reached.

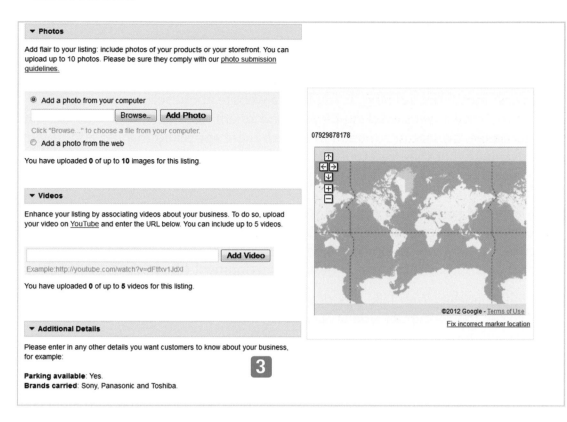

Understand website structure and indexing

The structure of your website is a powerful aspect of its online marketing. Have sections, grouped in some kind of order, all connected by the theme which categorises your business model (i.e. running, if you have a website about selling running shoes, cycling, if you have a website selling bicycles and so on). Well-structured websites are easier to manage, present information in a much more appealing manner and have the added advantage that they lead to easier indexing and greater online visitor time, all of which is great for your website's SEO status.

1 The layout of www.helpmyseo.com has been created specifically to help make its content more accessible. Section 1, for instance, labelled Web View, allows me to create content which comments on developments right across the Web which impact on SEO, social media and business development (the subjects I write about).

2 Section 2, labelled Web Talk, is podcasts, each approximately three minutes long. They cover the conceptual side of SEO, social media and marketing, and they are usually very topical.

3 Section 3, labelled Practical & Easy SEO Tips, is the core of the site's content. It contains SEO tips with a step-by-step approach. It is there to help webmasters rank their websites higher by applying specific SEO tips and staying abreast of SEO developments.

4 Section 4 is Inspiring Videos. Video marketing is important on the Web. It captures those who have little time to read and it can become a lot easier to share than long articles. In a multimedia-rich Web, not having video is akin to driving a car on three wheels.

! ALERT: It is important to remember that on the Web, time is short and attention spans suffer. Even the most dedicated of readers will baulk at having to read several hundred words each time they get to your website. This is why it is important to mix up the formats a little and provide something for everyone.

Use social sharing tools

Social media and social sharing is an incredibly important part of the means to drive traffic to websites. It also impacts on SEO. Here are a few of the social sharing tools you need to have implemented on your website.

1 Social sharing tools are installed using modules or APIs supplied by the different social sharing networks. Depending on the kind of programming which has been used on your website you may be able to simply install these yourself, or get your website developer to do it.

2 Apart from social sharing buttons for content, you should have the buttons of the social networks in which you are present and where people can follow you. These can range from Twitter and Facebook to Google Plus and Pinterest and any professional network you belong to. These are parts of your growing brand image and the selected crowd you draw around you.

3 You should also have an RSS (Real Simple Syndication) button which allows subscribers to click and subscribe so they can follow updates you make to your content in an RSS reader.

WHAT DOES THIS MEAN?

API: Stands for Application Programming Interface.
RSS: Stands for Real Simple Syndication.
Landing page: Any website page intended to capture online traffic and convert it into customers.

? DID YOU KNOW?

Google uses what it calls 'the social cue' as a strong signal for the ranking of websites. Content from your website which is shared and re-shared via social networks becomes a strong factor in the ranking of your website on the search results page.

Design your site for optimal SEO

The design of your landing pages is important because it is a ranking factor which affects the way Google assesses your website and the position it should have on search. The design of your landing page will also have a direct impact upon the visitor behaviour to your website. In this section we will look at five critical elements of good landing page design which can help your SEO.

1 *Ease of navigation*. Make sure that visitors on any page of your website find it easy to go to any other page.

2 *Obvious titles*. Make it easy to understand what each page is about.

> **ALERT:** Poor landing page design leads to high abandonment rates and low times spent on your website per visitor, both of which are a ranking metric Google takes into account.

3 *Social sharing buttons*. Allow your online visitors to interact with your content.

4 *Social network profile buttons*. Allow your visitors to follow you on the Web.

5 *Suggested content*. Offer your visitors the opportunity to discover more than just the content of that page.

> **HOT TIP:** Google uses accumulated data such as abandonment rates and online user behaviour to make a guess at how 'good' or 'bad' your website design is and then ranks your website accordingly.

> **HOT TIP:** It is worth spending time (and money) to create a clean visual style on your website which will help your online visitors enjoy the experience. Your site's ranking will benefit from that.

Use online tools to help your SEO

To help with your SEO we will use the Google Chrome browser because of its speed and stability. If you do not have it already go to www.google.com/chrome and download it. Once it is installed on your system go to http://goo.gl/rQeou. This is the Google Chrome Web Store. The SEO plugin you need is called 'SEO for Chrome' and it's free. Once you go to the page it will load automatically and all you have to do is click to install it on your browser.

1 The SEO plugin installs smoothly in the Google Chrome browser in the top right-hand side. To use it just go to any page of your website (the home page will do) or any competitor site you want to analyse and click on it.

2 The SEO plugin opens up on a pane containing data right over the website page which you are analysing. It gives you an instant overview of the SEO status of the

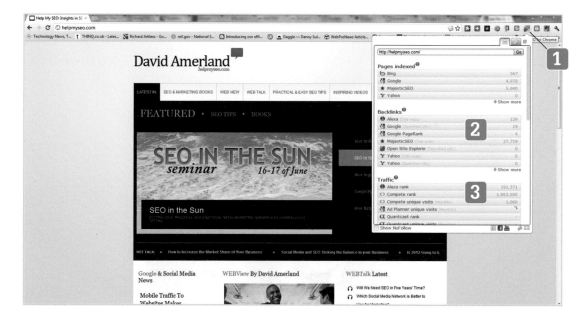

website and with each result it allows you to click and go deeper so you can actually drill down as far as you want and use it for more detail as your SEO skills and knowledge grow.

3 You will see that the information given to you by the SEO plugin is in three distinct sections: Pages indexed, Backlinks and Traffic. There are metrics in each section which directly impact upon each of these and they are all clickable and lead to other web pages where you can get more information. This is a great tool to use for a quick, at-a-glance check of the progress you are making in your SEO.

? DID YOU KNOW?
Your progress on the search engine rankings depends upon your own efforts and on the slip-ups of your competitors. The SEO plugin is the perfect spying glass for checking out what your competitors are doing.

HOT TIP: Gathering intelligence on competing sites allows you to determine when they are stepping up their own SEO efforts so you can take action.

Speed up the indexing of your pages

When you create content there is always a lag between the time it goes on your website and the time it is available through search. That time lag depends on many factors which you cannot control. Sometimes it may be no more than 48 hours and at other times it can take a week or even longer. Here are some ways you can speed up this process and get your pages indexed super-fast.

1 Go to Google Plus – https://plus.google.com/ – and use your Google Account to log in.

2 Create a profile and fill out the relevant data.

3 Make sure the data you input includes keywords which describe what you do and what your business is, and link from the text describing your business to your website.

4 Put in full descriptions about what your business is.

5 Put in links leading from your Google Plus profile to your website.

6 Add locations and cities. That's it. You're done. Now all you need to do each time you want your content to be indexed fast is share it on Google Plus.

? DID YOU KNOW?

Google looks at the speed of your website as a measure of the end-user experience. The search engine considers slow-loading pages as unlikely to deliver a great end-user experience and ranks them accordingly.

HOT TIP: Google Plus is Google's own social network and, as such, it is completely transparent to the Google bot. Content that gets shared there ends up in the Google Index about half an hour later. That's an incredible advantage for using it right there. In the past, in order to get that kind of indexing speed you needed to have a website like the BBC.

Increase how quickly your website loads

The speed at which your website loads is an important part of your SEO. Slow-loading websites frustrate the end-user. If Google has placed your site on search and it loads slowly, that frustration is then directed at Google. As a result Google now checks both server speeds and website loading speeds to make sure that websites are as light and fast as possible. In this section we will see how to check your website loading speed and how to improve it if necessary.

To take advantage of Google's website speed check go to https://developers.google.com/pagespeed/.

1 Enter your site's URL in the field box and press 'Analyze'.

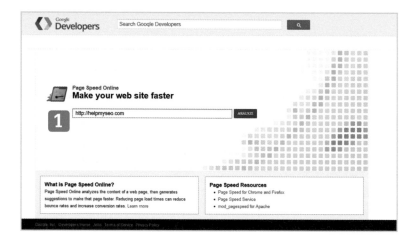

2 The analysis comes up with a numeric score out of 100. Anything above 55 is good, but there is always room for improvement. Bear in mind that even Google.com, when analysed, does not get a perfect 100.

3 Underneath the numeric score is a summary of suggested tasks, handily divided into High, Middle and Low priority. It is always best to scan things here and start, if possible, from the one you think you can do quickly.

4 Depending on when you last did the speed check you can also see the tasks you have fixed.

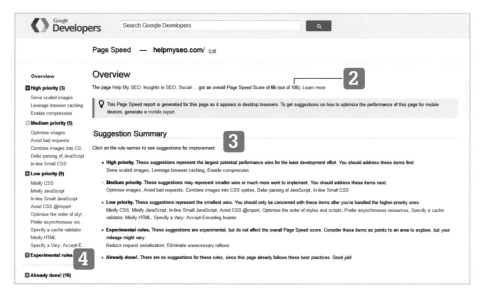

HOT TIP: Optimisation of your website's speed is often costly, particularly if there is coding involved. It is good practice to have set periods in the year when you look critically at your website's speed test and Google's suggestions and take action.

Prioritise website uptime

When your website is down (not available), SEO is affected. Downtime is one of the reasons websites drop from Google's first page. It is important to monitor your website's uptime in case there are problems.

There is a free website uptime monitoring service you can use called Hyperspin. Go to www.hyperspin.com/en/.

1 Put the URL of your website in the field box at the top of the page and click Test. You should get a report on your website's uptime.

2 Fill in your details and sign for a free account. Once a day you will get a report of your website's uptime delivered straight to your inbox. These reports are invaluable in assessing the quality of your hosting.

WHAT DOES THIS MEAN?
Downtime: This is when the server your website is served from is too slow to respond or is simply unavailable.

HOT TIP: A reliable server means that you have a reliable website, so make sure you choose a hosting company that is reputable and has great customer service. In the UK, United Hosting (www.unitedhosting.co.uk) has become a market leader.

Create SEO-friendly images

Images play a multiple role on a website. They ensure that the landing page design is visually appealing. They keep the visitor's eyes busy long enough for the content to start working, and they help your SEO. In this section we shall see the type of images which can be used and how they help exactly.

1 When it comes to images, size is important. Large images which are also optimised for the Web so that they load fast are deemed by Google to be SEO friendly because they are end-user friendly.

2 Images are invisible to the Google bot, so make sure they are described in detail using the alt txt (alternative text). If your website is based on a content management system (CMS) platform then you will be able to put in the alt txt description when you place your image in the text of your article. If you have a website which is not based on a CMS you will need to ask your developer to show you how to apply the alt txt when you load images.

3 Position the image prominently in relation to your article. Images which are halfway down the article or at the end are not given as much importance by the Google bot as when they are at the top, designed to catch the online visitor's eyes.

HOT TIP: Choose images that illustrate your website. Images should work so that they form a navigable map for your online visitors, directing them towards the text.

WHAT DOES THIS MEAN?
Alternative text: Alt text for short. This is the description of an image used to describe a picture to a search engine bot.

2 URLs and keywords

Introduction

Keywords are one of the core elements driving search and search ranking. Without them there would be little opportunity to optimise a website. You need keywords which are relevant to your business and a way to incorporate them in your search engine optimisation strategy.

Understand how a search query works

URL stands for uniform resource locator. It is the address of your website. Each page of your website has its own URL that distinguishes it from others on the World Wide Web. URLs are one of the core elements search engines use when they match a web page to a particular search query.

Perform this search query:

1 Type 'SEO help for my website'.

2 Note the number of competing pages for that search term.

3 In top position on the first page of Google you will probably see Helpmyseo.com.

4 In the second slot on the first page of Google you will probably see http://helpmyseo.com/seo-blog/174-seo-help-for-my-website.html.

5 Note the following:
   a   Protocol.
   b   Main domain name.
   c   Folder.
   d   Name of the page.

Learn how keywords work

Keywords are like a point-scoring system on search ranking. A perfect score is achieved when the keywords in the search query are matched by keywords in the domain name, page URL, page title and page content. Let's see how this stacks up on the page delivered to Google's #1 page for the search query 'SEO help for my website'.

1 The keywords here are in the domain name (SEO and help).

2 The exact keyword set is in the web page URL.

3 The search query is matched by the title of the page.

4 The opening sentence of the first paragraph also matches the search query.

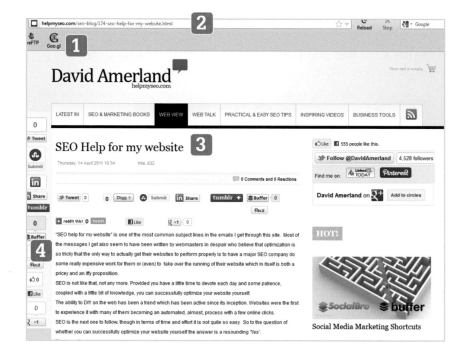

? DID YOU KNOW?

Where keywords appear on a page is very important. If a keyword appears at the end of a web page rather than at the top, for instance, its ability to help with ranking is diminished.

▶ SEE ALSO: Chapter 1 for other ranking factors which affect where your website will appear in Google Search.

Know how to implement keywords on your website

When you implement keywords to help your website rank higher on Google, incorporate these useful techniques.

1 Make sure the main keyword is present in the website description.

2 Ensure the main keywords are present in the domain name.

3 The main keywords should be present at the beginning of the web page.

4 There are two different pages from the same website ranking in the #1 and #2 position of the first page of Google for that particular search term.

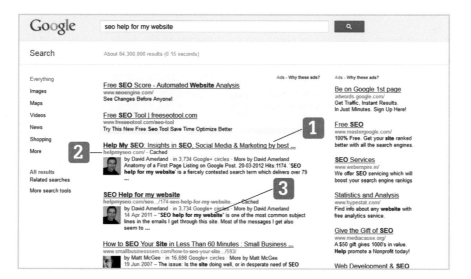

? DID YOU KNOW?
The longer the URL, the less effective the keywords in it become. Therefore, be aware of the length of your website's URL.

! ALERT: Creating URLs which repeat keywords is part of a banned SEO practice. If you do it the chances are that your website will be penalised by Google.

Implement keywords in web page titles

To successfully implement keywords in the titles of your website pages you need to have in place a structured approach which will inform your content-creation strategy. This will avoid unnecessary repetition and provide greater SEO focus.

1 Titles on the website revolve around specific topics.

2 Different titles help each other out (in this case around the keywords 'Social Media' and 'Marketing').

SEE ALSO: Chapter 3 for help with researching keywords.

3 The main keywords appear in different places in different titles.

4 There is a good mix of longer titles adding variety and content.

5 There is additional content on the same subject which does not repeat the keywords.

DID YOU KNOW?

Your page titles should read like book chapters. Each one should further help create an idea of what your website does and how.

Check what your competitors are doing

You keep an eye on your competition because it helps you fine-tune your own search engine optimisation strategy and you get to see what they do to maintain their presence in search. Tracking competitors starts with keywords.

1 Go to www.semrush.com.

2 Put in the URL of the competitor site you are checking.

3 Note the results of some of the top keywords they rank for and see that the traffic they get per month is displayed underneath.

? DID YOU KNOW?
If you click on each of the main keywords provided, you will also see their derivative keywords and the monthly search traffic which these keywords provide.

WHAT DOES THIS MEAN?

Potential ads buyers: This appears on the left-hand column of the semrush.com report and gives you a list of websites which buy ads for those keywords.

Backlinks: The number of websites linking back to your domain. semrush.com allows you to check on them through the click of the link labelled 'Backlinks Report' in the left-hand menu.

4 Note the country-specific Google Index.

5 You can use the Backlinks feature to see who links back to your competitor.

6 You can see the monthly traffic trend from a specific country.

Check backlinks to a competitor website

Backlinks still drive website authority and contribute to website ranking on the Google search page. A website that has a large number of high-quality backlinks will rank higher than a website that is equally well optimised but has no backlinks.

1 To check on a competitor website's backlinks go to www.opensiteexplorer.org/.

2 Type in the competitor website URL and press Search.

? DID YOU KNOW?
When you discover a competitor website's backlinks you also uncover part of their online marketing strategy. You understand where they market their content to and where they use other means, such as blog comments, to get links from.

3 The site's page authority is displayed as a number out of 100.

4 The domain's authority is displayed as a number out of 100.

5 The total number of links will be displayed.

6 The links and the anchor keytext will also be listed below.

WHAT DOES THIS MEAN?

Page rank: Google is transitioning from a page rank (PR) ranking, which values your site from 1 to 7, to an authority ranking, which values it out of 100. PR will remain but it will be an indicator and little more.

Optimise your website using online tools

There are free online tools from Google which will help you optimise your website and improve performance. To take advantage of them you will need to use your Google Account.

1 Go to https://developers.google.com/pagespeed/ and press Analyze. It takes a minute or two and then the results will be displayed below.

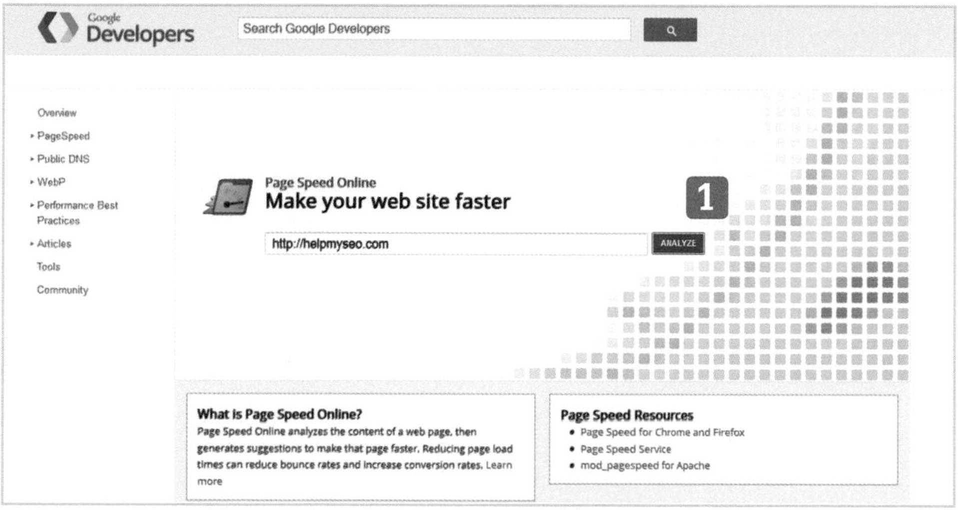

2 Google's optimising tool will deliver its verdict in a website score out of 100 and colour-coded tasks.

a High priority – to be seen to as soon as possible.

b Medium priority – that may take more work to implement.

c Low priority – which should be last on your list.

d Experimental rules – which usually means optional.

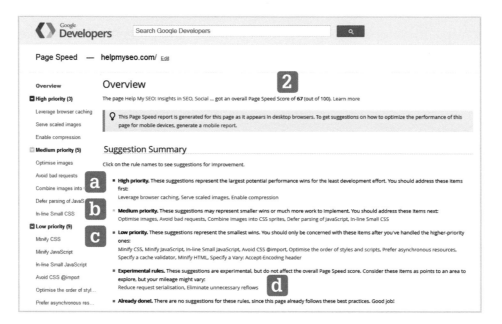

Use metadata for better ranking

Metadata is loosely interpreted as 'data about data' and it is used at website structure level to help search engines better understand, index and rank the content you create on your website. There are three key elements you need to be aware of when you use metatags on your website:

a   *Title*. The title of your page is incredibly important when it comes to search queries.

b   *Description*. The description of your page is important because, on the search results page itself, it's what human visitors see.

c   *Keywords*. The keywords you use in your page title and page content also play a crucial part in ranking.

ALERT: When you use keywords which match search queries make sure that they really belong in your web page content. Forcing them there to trick Google Search will result in your website being penalised.

SEE ALSO: Know how to implement keywords on your website, earlier in this chapter.

Incorporate rich snippets

Rich snippets is the name Google gives to the title and description which appear on search, along with your website's URL, in response to a search query. The image here shows an example of a rich snippet.

1 The description directly under the title of the website's page on the search results page is the snippet.

2 There is some additional data which goes into the snippet description which does not appear on search but which Google indexes.

3 Rich snippets affect the searchers' decision to click on a particular listing on the search results page.

- The description will appear under the title.
- The website page has been authenticated through a Google Account in Google Plus.
- The website authorship is verified through a Google Account.

SEE ALSO: To see how a rich snippet appears on Search, go to www.google.com/webmasters/tools/richsnippets.

? DID YOU KNOW?
Google uses the profile you create in Google Plus to help authenticate website content.

WHAT DOES THIS MEAN?
Click Through Rate (CTR): The number of people who click on a particular listing on the Google search results page. It is a ranking signal Google looks at.

Link your website to your Google Plus Account

When you link your website to your Google Plus Account you increase the authenticity of your content and the strength of the signal Google gets from you.

1 Create a Google Plus profile at https://plus.google.com.

2 Fill out your Google Plus profile linking to your website in the right-hand column.

3 Add your website in the description (this is not necessary but it is good SEO).

4 Get a Google Plus badge from https://developers.google.com/+/plugins/badge/ and add the badge to your website.

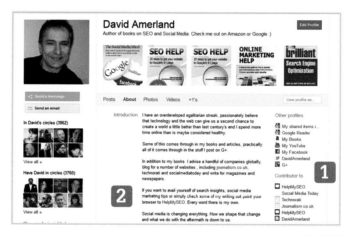

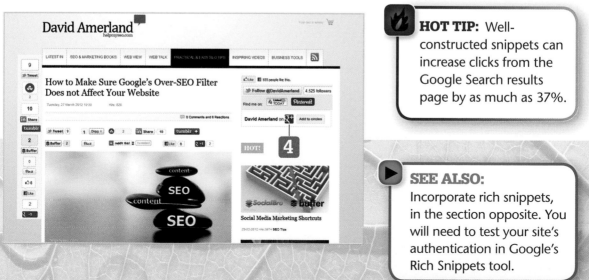

HOT TIP: Well-constructed snippets can increase clicks from the Google Search results page by as much as 37%.

SEE ALSO: Incorporate rich snippets, in the section opposite. You will need to test your site's authentication in Google's Rich Snippets tool.

3 Keywords and content

Introduction

Keywords are important for search engines and they are part of the core which helps power your website's ranking. When it comes to the content of your website your keywords can never be left to chance.

Research keywords for content

There are several ways to research the best keywords. It's best to log into your Google Account from the outset here. Once you've done that, go to http://goo.gl/8AkZU.

 DID YOU KNOW?
Local search volumes (the number of people searching for a particular query) and global search volumes for particular search queries are different. The information allows you to more precisely target online visitors to your site.

1 Input your search term.

2 Add your website.

3 Choose the best category.

4 Tick Only show ideas closely related to my search term.

5 Choose region and language for greater localisation.

HOT TIP: Google is far from impartial when suggesting terms. Make sure that you keep your keyword groups as tightly clustered as possible by always ticking the Only show ideas closely related to my search term box in the Google Keyword Suggestion tool.

Group your keywords for better ranking

The Google Keywords Research tool will give you a long list of keywords relevant to your business and industry. It's worth remembering that not all keywords are equal. Some will be more relevant than others and you will need to do a little sorting to get them to work for you.

1 Choose your keywords group according to word groups.

2 Group them by monthly volume on global search.

3 Group them by monthly volume on local search.

Keyword	Competition	Global Monthly Searches	Local Monthly Searches
seo ▾	Medium	9,140,000	1,000,000

Keyword ideas (100)   1 - 50 of 100 ☑ < >

Keyword	Competition	Global Monthly Searches	Local Monthly Searches
seo london ▾	Medium	49,500	40,500
seo uk ▾	Medium	60,500	49,500
seo manchester ▾	Medium	12,100	12,100
seo company uk ▾	Medium	18,100	12,100
seo services uk ▾	Medium	12,100	8,100
seo agency ▾	Medium	49,500	18,100
free seo report ▾	Medium	3,600	1,300
seo consultancy ▾	Medium	74,000	22,200
seo leeds ▾	Medium	4,400	4,400
seo costs ▾	Medium	14,800	5,400
seo training course ▾	Medium	12,100	3,600
seo courses ▾	Medium	40,500	8,100
seo agencies ▾	High	40,500	18,100
uk seo ▾	Medium	60,500	49,500
seo edinburgh ▾	Medium	2,900	2,900
seo company london ▾	Medium	18,100	14,800
uk seo company ▾	Medium	18,100	12,100
seo glasgow ▾	Medium	5,400	5,400
seo nottingham ▾	Low	1,900	1,900
seo consultants ▾	Medium	60,500	18,100
seo sheffield ▾	Medium	1,600	1,600
seo services london ▾	Medium	5,400	4,400

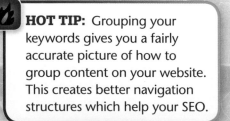

HOT TIP: Grouping your keywords gives you a fairly accurate picture of how to group content on your website. This creates better navigation structures which help your SEO.

Manage your website navigation

The navigation of your website is an important factor for your SEO. It also helps human visitors find content which is relevant and grouped in a certain order.

1 'SEO' appears in the navigation.

2 'SEO' appears in a central section.

3 It appears as a keyword in titles.

4 It is used as a keyword in main articles.

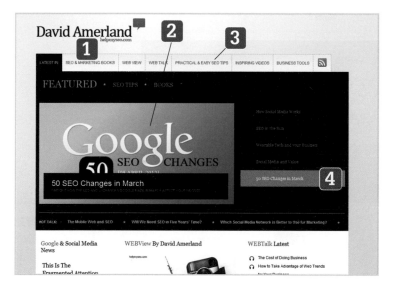

🔥 **HOT TIP:** Create navigation headings which readily define the section of your content. This will allow you to build up relevant articles in sections of your website and boost its ranking in search.

⚠ **ALERT:** Always make sure that your content sections truly reflect the content you place in them. Disparities frequently trigger Google filters, even on websites which do not set out to game the system.

Boost your website's SEO importance

There is one easy way to help boost your website's SEO: through better indexing of pages and better presentation of content.

1 The navigation tabs at the top of the website represent sections of its content.

2 These sections are replicated at the bottom using text navigation links.

3 Text navigation links allow a much more detailed breakdown of content.

HOT TIP: Create navigational links at the bottom of your site and they act as an easy guide for human visitors as well as search engines.

DID YOU KNOW? Google and other search engines frequently experience indexing problems from website navigational tabs. Text links make sure that all your website content is found and indexed.

Create a website SEO map

Your website's SEO map is supported by the keywords and the keyword groups you have researched. To make them work for you, they need to be arranged in a funnel effect. This is where the map comes in.

The corresponding stages of your SEO map are:

- website content (groups of keywords)
- keywords used
- website design
- landing page design.

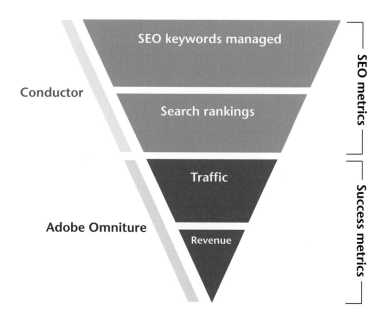

Use linking strategies for website traffic

Linking strategies help create better traffic to all your pages and better traffic to your website. By implementing a site-wide linking strategy you help both human visitors and search bots.

1 In the case of Helpmyseo.com, every article links to Related Content.

2 The pages are linked to add value to the existing article.

The Mercedes ad above has over nine million views at the time of writing. The car makers showed us a new car but they also showed us the challenge of making the ad for the new car and in doing so they explained why it was a challenge and the kind of ingenious solution they came up with in order to meet the challenge.

You notice they did not try to sell us the car. Instead they made us virtual partners in the making of the ad and by doing so they 'cleverly' subverted our natural resistance to advertising. But that's not all they did. They showed us what is possible when technology and passion come up against the necessity to work. They made us realise just how difficult their job is how skilled they are at overcoming its challenges and, oh yes, they made us aware of the Hydrogen Fuel-Cell technology, zero emissions car by Mercedes.

Each time it is employed social media achieves three fundamental qualities which change in their consistency according to the setting and situation: Transparency, Accountability and Empowerment. It strips away the layers which we have become accustomed to hide behind and reveals the inner workings underneath and the moment it does that it also allows us to wholly participate in the exercise, assess the underlying logic and analyse its effectiveness. This way it spreads awareness, knowledge and a much different way of making decisions than anything we have had before.

This cuts across the board, from ad-making to marketing, to creating a law or making a cake. What we then choose to do with this increased knowledge and awareness is exactly what has the power to change everything.

Related Content   **1**

How to Take Advantage of Web Trends for Your Business (Podcast)
The Politics of Value
Social Media Marketing Shortcuts   **2**
Two Social Media Created Stars
The Jackie Chan Factor in Social Media
Five Social Media Marketing Lessons Taught by Batman
The Uniqueness of 'You' in a Social Media Environment
Can Social Media Democratize the Lawmaking Process?
Interest Graph Marketing is More Important than Social Graph Targeting

? DID YOU KNOW?
You need to keep careful track of your existing content so that you can always add relevant links at the bottom of new content.

! ALERT: The practice of including links directly from the body text of each page to another page is falling into disuse. Google considers it a poor user experience and although it does not specifically frown upon it, it is no longer best practice.

Create a linking strategy

Linking to sites other than your own used to be considered bad form, because it led to a dilution of website PageRank (PR) and led visitors away from your website. This has now changed, but you need to know how best to use linking.

1 A single link to an external site is included within the body text of the article.

2 A number of links to related content are placed at the bottom of the article.

3 A number of links to external websites are placed at the bottom of the article.

HOT TIP: In order to keep visitors on your website it is wise to have links to other websites opening on a separate web page.

DID YOU KNOW?
When you link from your website to other websites with related content you increase the relevance of your own website and this helps its ranking on search.

Create snippets which help your website visitors

Snippets are the descriptive paragraphs which show what a page does on the Google search results page. They have become incredibly important for driving traffic to a website.

1 The search query 'Why are people poor' delivers HelpMySEO on the first page of Google at #2.

2 The two-line description (snippet) of the page took 15 minutes to get right.

3 There are keywords (in bold here) in the description of the snippet which are also reflected in the title of the page and the search query.

HOT TIP: Your snippet writing should never be an afterthought. You need to write short, compelling snippets which best describe what the content of the website page is about and which tie in with its title.

DID YOU KNOW?
A well-written snippet can lead up to 35% of extra web traffic to your website.

ALERT: Never give in to the temptation to write a snippet which does not reflect the content of your website. There is a Google filter for that which will result in a Google penalty.

Use long-tail keywords

Long-tail keywords fell out of favour with the Google Panda update of March 2011. They have since come back into use as Google has updated Google Instant to take them into account.

 Google Instant now supports long-tail keywords in search suggestions.

2 The Google Search results page pre-loads relevant pages based on long-tail keywords.

3 This makes it worthwhile to optimise content for long-tail keywords.

4 Long-tail keyword content can achieve a high ranking more easily.

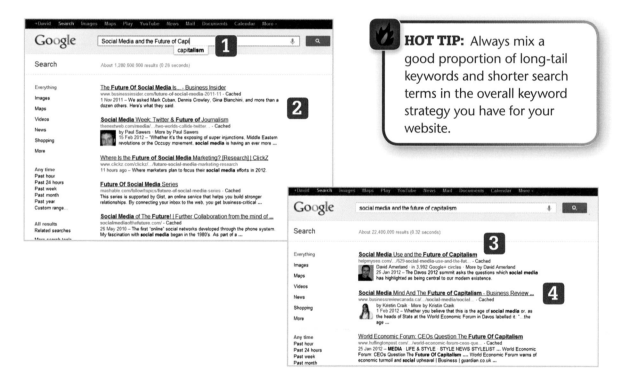

HOT TIP: Always mix a good proportion of long-tail keywords and shorter search terms in the overall keyword strategy you have for your website.

? DID YOU KNOW?

Long-tail keywords are not contested as heavily as more popular, much shorter search terms.

WHAT DOES THIS MEAN?

Long-tail keywords: Keywords which are longer descriptive sentences or expressions and are therefore less frequently used by those carrying out a search. They have a lower contention ratio and can help get your website to the first page of Google, quickly.

Estimate your website ranking for specific keywords

It always helps to know where your site ranks for specific search queries and keywords. Luckily there is a free tool to help you here.

1 Log onto Google's Webmaster Tools using your Google Account (www.google.com/webmasters/tools).

2 Navigate to Your site on the web.

3 Click on Search queries.

4 The search queries your site ranks for will appear alongside average rank.

Use keywords naturally

Prior to the Google Panda update, keyword density in SEO was calculated as a percentage of keywords per other words in the text. Now it is best to have as natural a writing style as possible with a few considerations we will see now.

1 Use keywords in the title of your articles.

2 Use keywords as soon as you can in picture captions or text.

3 Use keywords in your page URL.

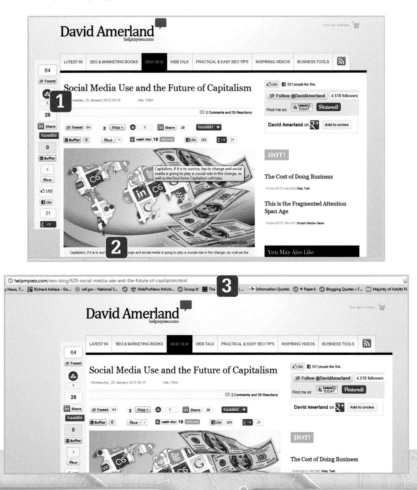

4 Content and SEO

Introduction

Content is still king on the Web, but in order for it to work it is no longer possible for a website to simply have content. You now need to have the right kind of content.

Know what is spam content

Content which is created with the specific intention of attracting search engine attention and helping a website to rank higher, but is of little or no value to human visitors, is considered to be spam.

1 Spam uses strong repetition of keywords in a lot of text.

2 This enforces the signal to search engines to rank those keywords.

3 The same applies with links introduced in text.

```
nand seo, LinxBot megaupload , auto backlink bomb download, top backlink building software reviews, nohandseo software, NOHANDSSEO vs
scrapebox, no hands seo free, banned no hands seo, no hand seo softwear, f, auto backlink software, tutorial auto blacklink, How to use No
Hands SEO software, Tweeternaire review, No Hands SEO megaupload, free squidoo linkposting software#q=free automatic high pr link building
software, "no hands seo" use approve , no hands seo bl     t, no hands seo#pq=no hands seo, SEO applications, seo software forum, nohandsseo
tutorial, Tweeternaire, linxbot tutorial, download smf     n txt backlink, "free linxbot", scrape High PR websites software, no hands seo
tutorial, What is "No Hands SEO"?, Submit and Share yo   tes, news and stories, Submit and Share your sites, news and stories, Submit and
Share your sites, news and stories, Submit and Share your sites, news and stories, no hands seo rapidshare, seo rapidshare, nohand seo
review, [Get] NO HANDS SEO, get tweeternaire download, auto backlink bomb review, forum links for no hands seo, "Auto Backlink Bomb"
hotfile, tweeternaire filesonic, [get]no hands seo mediafile, back link bot, mediafire backlink software, No_Hands_SEO.rar, linxbot vs
scrapebox, "No hands seo", No Hands SEO rar, no hands seo rapidshare download, TweeterNaire#sclient=psy-ab, earn money with tweeternaire,
tweeternaire backlinks, TweeterNaire, buy linxbot, I used tweeternaire and my account was banned, backlink software rar, no handsseo video
tutoials, TweeterNaire download, no hands seo download blogspot, high PR SEO Forum list, seo software auto backlink bomb rar, Auto Backlink
Bomb rar, auto backlink bomb mediafire, seo software link building -directory, NOHANDSEO, best link building hands free, Backlink Building
And Pinging Software mediafire, no hands seo filesonic, AutoBacklinkBomb      get No Hands SEO, auto seo free, filesonic seo software,
linxbot negative reviews, No hands SEO software, mp hands seo revioew#scl    psy-ab, no hands seo megaupload, no hands seo forum, the best
link building software that actually works, download:nohandseo +.rar, lin    download, auto approve list no hands seo, no hands seo vs
scrapebox, auto comment bomb hotfile, Free no hands SEO, No Hands SEO filesonic rapidshare megaupload, No Hands SEO rapidshare, mediafire
seo link building software, linx bot download#sclient=psy-ab, LinxBot.rar -filestube, forum hands no seo, no hand seo review , Auto Backlink
Bomb rapidshare, auto backlink bomb rapidshare, autobacklinkbomb download, download no hands seo, no hand seo opinion, LinxBot latest
version rapidshare, LinxBot free download, SEO hand on tutorial, download backlinks spftware.rar, seo backlink bomb.rar, AUTO BACK LINKS
SOFTWARE mediafire, yahoo, how to use no hands seo, auto backlink bomb medIAFIRE LINKS, autobacklink bomb mediafire links, No Hands SEO â,
autobacklinkbomb warez, backlink bomb hotfile, auto backlink bomb hotfile, best auto backlink program, best wordpress themes, SEO auto link
bot, download nohandseo, seo softwares, backlink filesonic, best backlink software, best seo software, Auto backlink Bomb, review nohandseo,
"auto link bot", , autolinkbot review, "no hands seo.rar", backlink+megaupload, "autobacklinkbomb.rar", backlink mediafire, auto backlink,
smf backlink, backlink megaupload, seo filesonic, autolink bot, profile multithread seo, tweeternaire mediafire, the best automated backlink
seo software, "backlinksoftware.rar", index/of autolinkbot.zip, autobacklinkbomb no hand seo, free high pr backlinks list, tweeternaire
warez, backlink + rapidshare download, i want link building free software, auto "twitter marketing software", link building mediafire,
"Submit and Share your sites, news and stories" "Submit and Share your sites, news and stories" "Submit and Share your sites, news and
```

out available a fantastic exercise routine a lot sooner than you imagine. This post includes numerous ideas that could show you to improve your workout in a short amount of time, which enable it to <u>pay day loan</u> you stay healthy and keep the kitchen connoisseur.

3

To assist you to recover <u>loan</u> coming from a tricky exercise routine, try out offering the muscle groups exercise the next day. You want to do this softly, about 20 on the weight that one could elevate on one occasion. Try to do 25 repetitions in 2 packages. Choosing this, you'll have additional blood and nutrients sent to the muscle groups for quicker fix.

Climbing is a terrific way to stay fit while not having to expend every day <u>fast cash loans</u> a

? DID YOU KNOW?
Google calls content like this webspam to distinguish it from email spam.

! ALERT: Never engage in any kind of content creation like this. Google has specific filters in place which will drop your website rankings.

Understand Google's Panda update

Google's Panda update targets websites which deliver a poor end-user experience through low-quality content. To address this, websites changed their design to incorporate elements of navigation that included a greater number of better graphics and more links.

1 There are clearer tabbed navigation menus at the top.

2 Additional navigation can be found through graphics.

3 Multimedia links are useful.

4 Eye-catching graphics make it a more interesting experience for visitors.

> **? DID YOU KNOW?**
> Google's Panda update hit hard websites which had a lot of content but poor navigation and low-quality content.

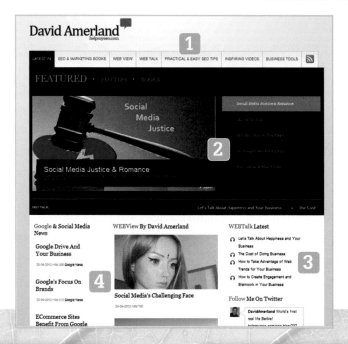

> **🔥 HOT TIP:** Natural speech is now back on track for providing the best results in terms of indexed text which is of high quality.

> **⚠ ALERT:** When you create landing pages, those which have more pictures than text and links are deemed by Google to deliver a poorer end-user experience and may be penalised.

Use Webmaster Tools for higher ranking

The Search queries section of Google Webmaster Tools can provide you with the vital clues and information you need to help improve your website's ranking.

1 The number of queries your site was served for.

2 The number of impressions resulting from the queries.

3 The number of clicks delivered.

4 The search queries that were used.

5 The number of impressions for each query.

6 The average ranking of your site for that query.

	Impressions	Clicks	CTR	Avg. position
froogle	12,000	16	0%	8.1
google places login	6,500	<10	-	11
"powered by fox contact" s	3,000	<10	-	340
blackhat seo google penalty	2,500	<10	-	9.4
"powered by fox contact" w	2,000	<10	-	230
"powered by fox contact" n	2,000	<10	-	280
seo help	1,600	<10	-	13

HOT TIP: Google Webmaster Tools now delivers more accurate website ranking for specific keywords than before.

? DID YOU KNOW?
Many of the keywords which deliver traffic to your website no longer appear in Google Analytics. Webmaster Tools has become necessary to plug the gap.

Use Google Analytics to help with content

Google Analytics provides valuable insights regarding the way your website's content appeals to your online visitors. Through it you can see:

1. The number of page views that were served to your online visitors.

2. The number of unique pages that were served to your online visitors.

3. The average time visitors spent on your site.

4. The number of visitors who see only one page on your site.

5. The number of times these pages are the last pages a visitor sees.

HOT TIP: The bounce rate is always a better indicator of a website's stickiness than the exit rate.

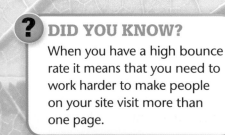

DID YOU KNOW? When you have a high bounce rate it means that you need to work harder to make people on your site visit more than one page.

ALERT: When the average time visitors spend on your website is less than 90 seconds, it will count against your search ranking.

Avoid Google's spam signature trap

Even legitimate websites can trip Google's spam website filters and be penalised. That's because these filters are automated and look for a specific 'signature' in a website. Here's what to do to avoid creating that signature.

1. Make sure content is illustrated with a relevant photograph.

2. Make your content 400 words or longer.

3. Have your post surrounded by relevant content.

4. Have additional links to relevant content in your post.

5. Have matching relevance in other content on your website.

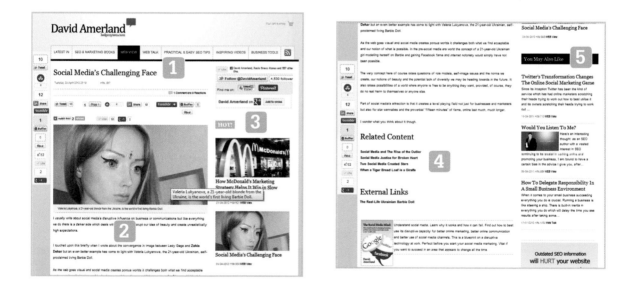

? DID YOU KNOW?
Website content which consistently falls below the 400-word rule begins to look suspiciously like spam.

! ALERT: Pages containing short content, poor graphics and Google ads all over the place are just some of the triggers which Google looks for when deciding that a website is possible webspam.

Make sure your website content 'tells a story'

Websites which are comprised of just bits and pieces put together without much thought rarely succeed in converting visitors to customers. Their SEO also suffers.

1 Arrange your content so that it tells instantly what you do.

2 Support it with high-quality graphics.

3 Use corroborative content that supports the main pages.

4 Use additional main content of equally high quality.

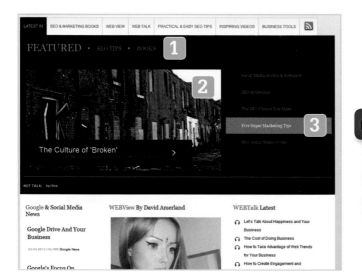

HOT TIP: The quality of your graphics can now help your SEO. Use large images, optimised for the Web, and make sure you label them properly with suitable keywords.

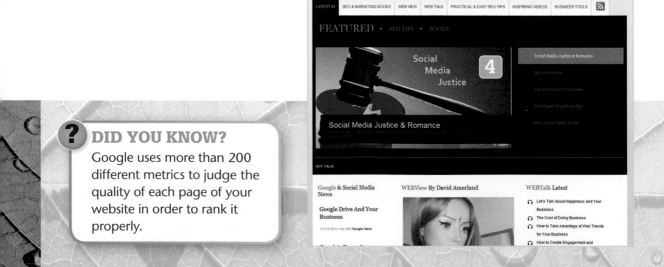

? DID YOU KNOW?
Google uses more than 200 different metrics to judge the quality of each page of your website in order to rank it properly.

Plan your website's content

Planning the content of your website is an important step in your content creation plan. To help you put it together you need to look at your home page layout and divide it into sections.

1 Use sections which appeal to your core customers first and then increase your site's appeal by creating sections which also appeal to customers peripheral to your core.

2 Use your strongest visuals to entice non-core customers to stay on your site.

3 Add multimedia in the form of podcasts or video to capture online visitors who may be short of time.

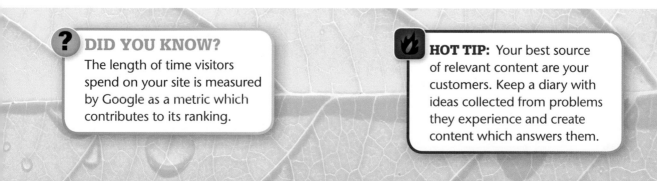

? DID YOU KNOW?
The length of time visitors spend on your site is measured by Google as a metric which contributes to its ranking.

🔥 HOT TIP: Your best source of relevant content are your customers. Keep a diary with ideas collected from problems they experience and create content which answers them.

See your content on the Web

Learn how to use your content better by seeing just how it is indexed on the Web and how it appears in search.

1️⃣ The search query 'Social Media's Challenging Face' has more than 200 million competing pages.

2️⃣ Search delivers HelpMySEO.com on the first page of Google.

3️⃣ Image Search delivers the image from the article on HelpMySEO on Google's second row of images against over 152 million others.

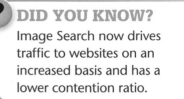

? DID YOU KNOW?
Image Search now drives traffic to websites on an increased basis and has a lower contention ratio.

🔥 HOT TIP: By adding a good-quality image to your article and optimising it and labelling it with keywords pertinent to the article, you increase its chances of coming up high on Image Search.

WHAT DOES THIS MEAN?
Contention ratio: The number of other web pages which contest with your website for a first page on Google listing.

Establish a content creation strategy

A content creation strategy helps you create content which echoes web trends and helps generate more web traffic for you. Its preparation consists of very specific steps.

- Make your content comprehensive, covering everything your visitors need.
- Do your research in keywords and subject.
- Accumulate resources which you can share.
- Prepare to spread your content through social networks.
- Do not make your content into an ad for your business.

HOT TIP: Use the steps in this section to create a content creation strategy which fits in with the sections of your website.

HOT TIP: Create content which is truly useful to those who come to your website – usually content which answers a specific question or solves a problem.

Avoid duplicate content on your website

Duplicate content on your website can undermine much of the SEO power of what you are building and drop your website rankings in search.

1 Make similar content in different sections of your website, different.

2 Create content which is defined by length and style.

3 Create titles which help differentiate similar content.

Claim your website content so it cannot be copied

Prove your website content is your own to a search engine and you can guarantee that even if it is copied and used elsewhere, you will not suffer.

1. Use your Google Account to update your Google Plus profile and link to your website.

2. Close the loop by linking from your website back to Google Plus with one of the official, pre-made badges.

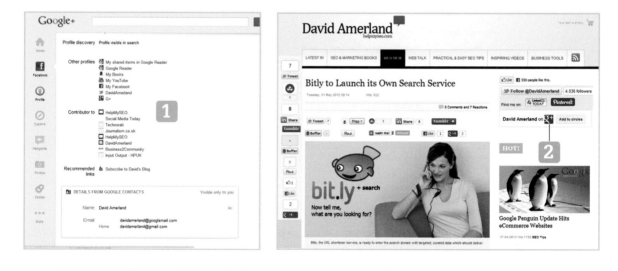

HOT TIP: Verify your website through your Google Plus profile and Google knows that the content is yours even if it is scraped so potential duplicate content issues may not arise.

ALERT: You are allowed to claim ownership of only one website this way. If you happen to own several or contribute to several you will need to choose which one to link to.

? DID YOU KNOW?
Claiming ownership of your website and its content this way helps identify you in search with a thumbnail of the picture you have used on your Google Plus profile.

WHAT DOES THIS MEAN?
Scraping: This is when website content is stolen using an automated program commonly called a scraper.

Verify you have claimed your website's content

Check to see that your website ownership claim through your Google Plus account and Google Plus badge has worked.

1 Go to www.google.com/webmasters/tools/richsnippets and input your home page URL.

2 Check to see if authorship has been recognised.

3 See if your thumbnail comes up.

? DID YOU KNOW?
Verifying your website boosts its ranking in search by increasing its authority.

🔥 HOT TIP: Authority rank is a new metric Google is experimenting with. It will define the way websites are assessed and ranked in search in the future on an ever increasing basis.

Refresh your website content in the Google Index

Refresh the content of your website stored in the Google Index whenever you want and benefit from an increased number of keywords performing well in Google Search.

1 Go to Google Plus.

2 Create a short post there which uses some of the keywords of the content you want to promote.

3 Add the URL of the web page you want to promote.

4 Google will find the link and follow it back to your website, picking up the new content and refreshing what is in its Index about your website.

? DID YOU KNOW?
Posting your content on Google Plus gets it indexed in the Google Index within a 20-minute window.

🔥 HOT TIP: Google is great at indexing links. Pages on your website which have links pointing to other pages on your website which have related content will rank higher than standalone pages which have no links at all.

Socialise your website's content

Share your website's content across different social networks and you help your website to be found more easily, rank higher and be better indexed by the Google bot.

1 Include on your website some social network buttons which will help your website visitors share the content they find through their favourite social network.

2 Include these social sharing buttons in as many locations as you can so that content can be shared in a much easier manner.

3 Include social network buttons which link to your profile so your website's visitors can choose to follow you.

? DID YOU KNOW? Social networks are scanned by the search engine bots looking for a 'social signal' which contains content from your website.

HOT TIP: Share your website's content on different social networks and not only do you increase the possibility of your website ranking higher but you will also attract new visitors.

! ALERT: Socialising your website's content in each social network requires a different tone and 'voice' for each. Their demographics are different and you need to be able to adapt.

5 SEO strategies and your business

Introduction

Search engine optimisation works best when it is part of what your business does rather than an extra bolt-on you use from time to time.

Create an SEO strategy for your business

A strategy implies that SEO activity for your business happens with specific targets in mind. To achieve this you need to display your website content in a way which creates a clear picture of what your business does and how, and this requires additional text-link, website navigation.

1 Group your content under items which are actionable by your online visitors.

2 Highlight your products.

3 Use keywords in your link text.

4 Provide an additional means to capture website visitors.

ALERT: Create text links as an additional navigational aid and not the main one. Keep the number to around a maximum of 100. Google has recently started to index more than 100 text links per page but it still prefers a lower number.

DID YOU KNOW?
Search engine bots love to crawl text-based navigational links. When you have such links on your website you make it easier for search engines as well as for human visitors to find and better index your content.

HOT TIP: The success of your SEO strategy depends upon your ability to distil your business into simple, actionable and informational text-based navigational links.

Automate your SEO strategy

In the SEO world very few things are truly 'automated' and those which are, sooner or later, will run into trouble as SEO requirements change. The way to get around this is to know which parts of your SEO strategy you can safely automate and which ones you need to closely manage yourself.

1 Use an RSS feed to automatically publicise content on your website the moment it is dropped in.

2 Employ social media sharing buttons and use them straight from the content you place on your website.

3 Use Buffer (http://bufferapp.com) to automate the number of Tweets you release throughout the day.

HOT TIP: Social media-automated aids like Buffer also come with an on-board analytics dashboard which helps you see the number of clicks your posts have generated.

? DID YOU KNOW?

Your SEO strategy requires you to know the best time of day to send a Tweet so that it reaches the greatest possible number of people in your target audience.

Set up Google Alerts

You need to monitor your website if you are to have an idea where your content appears. Google allows you to set up a monitoring search which will automatically keep track of the mentions of your website across the entire Web. For this you will need your Google Account login and password.

1 Go to www.google.com/alerts.

2 Fill in the search query field with the term you want to look for.

3 Use the drop-down boxes to refine what you want to look for.

4 Look at some of the results which Google finds for you.

5 Press Create Alert.

Google Alerts **1**

Search query:	David Amerland **2**
Result type:	Everything
How often:	Once a day **3**
How many:	Only the best results
Deliver to:	davidamerland@gmail.com

CREATE ALERT   Manage your alerts

5

There are no recent results for your search query. Below is a sample of the type of results you will get.

Web   5 new results for **David Amerland**

DavidAmerland
David Amerland is the best-selling author of a number of books on search engine optimization, marketing and the new, wired, age. May. 2 ...
www.davidamerland.com/

David Amerland | Social Media Today
Bio: **David Amerland** is the author of the best-selling 'SEO Help: 20 steps to get your website to Google's #1 page'. His latest book: The Social Media Mind: How ...
socialmediatoday.com/user/71457

Help My SEO: Insights in SEO, Social Media & Marketing by best ...
David Amerland. Latest In · SEO & Marketing Books · WEB View · WEB Talk · Practical & Easy SEO Tips · Inspiring Videos .... WEBView by **David Amerland** ...
helpmyseo.com/

4
David Amerland (@DavidAmerland) on Twitter
Sign up for Twitter to follow **David Amerland** (**@DavidAmerland**). Techno-optimist and best-selling author of books on SEO and Social Media. I tweet a lot on all ...
twitter.com/davidamerland

David Amerland | Facebook
Join Facebook to connect with **David Amerland** and others you may know. Facebook gives people the power to share and makes the world more open and ...
www.facebook.com/david.amerland

? DID YOU KNOW?
You can create up to 1,000 alerts and Google will deliver a summary of the results straight to your inbox.

HOT TIP: When you set up your alerts do not limit yourself to your website name. Set up alerts which use search terms in your industry and keep tabs of what your competitors are doing.

Carry out a vanity search

Vanity searches, as the name implies, have to do with searches which involve your website or company name. Vanity searches allow you to see just how far your online marketing is reaching by checking to see where the search term you are checking appears.

1 Go to Google.co.uk, make sure you are not in the personalised results and input the search term you need to check.

2 Look at the number of pages which come up.

3 Check the direct results on the first three or four pages.

HOT TIP: When conducting a vanity search it is also advisable to go to Google's Image Search by clicking on the Images link at the top of Google Search. This will show you just which images from your website have been indexed and where they are.

? DID YOU KNOW?

When you do a vanity search you can also uncover potential marketing allies by seeing where mentions of your website and its content have been made.

Use social media to boost your SEO

The sharing and re-sharing of your website's content across social media networks produces a signal, frequently called a 'social signal'. This signal is seen by search engines and is factored in their assessment of a website's ranking.

1 Always start off with a social network where you have an established presence.

2 Share your content using targeted keywords and an introduction designed to elicit some engagement.

3 Link to the content leading to your website.

> **HOT TIP:** The social signal of your content is boosted with the number of re-shares it gets and the number of 'Likes' it gets.

> **DID YOU KNOW?**
> When you place content in a social network its average lifespan is about 90 minutes. After that you will need to post fresh content or repost the previous one, at least once more.

> **ALERT:** You should not get into the habit of reposting the same content all the time as your content will be viewed as spamming and you will lose some of your followers.

Link up social media profiles

When you promote your website through social media profiles, time is always against you. There are some easy ways to help you save time by interlinking social media profiles so that when you post to one, others are updated automatically.

1 Go to your Twitter account and log in.

2 Go to your profile and make sure it is optimised with a description which contains some of the keywords you need.

3 Link your Twitter profile updates to your Facebook ones by authorising access of one for the other (it can be revoked at any time).

ALERT: When you link social media accounts the updates are the same for both. It is important to remember that the demographics of social networks are different from one to the other and you need to strike the right tone in your posts.

DID YOU KNOW?
The messages you post in different social networks will reach their widest audience at different times. For best results you need to take this into account when you have linked your social network profiles and double your daily post rate to compensate.

Create content for high-volume traffic

Seeing lots of online visitors coming to your website every day creates a sense of excitement and also provides your online business with great exposure. Your website's content on its own will not help you achieve this day after day without a little help from the odd, highly popular post.

1 Find a subject which is trending across the Web and which you can write about by stretching your website's subject matter a little.

2 Use the trending keywords in the description of images and captions.

3 Use keywords contextually in the article body.

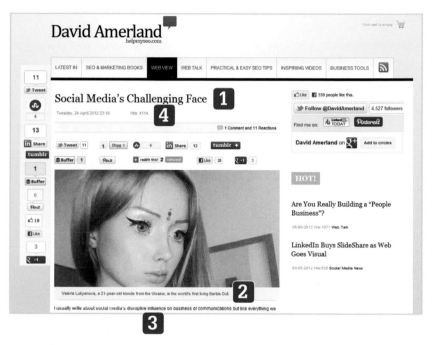

4 Gauge the effectiveness of your traffic for future reference through a view counter or your Google Analytics.

🔥 HOT TIP: You can find trending topics across the Web by looking at the Yahoo service for Trending Topics across the Web: http://news.yahoo.com/blogs/trending-now/. It takes some patience before you find one you can work with. When you do, you must seize the opportunity.

⚠ ALERT: News jacking works best at bringing you content when you can actually tie it to what you do, no matter how tenuous the connection may be. Content that bears no connection with what you do may bring you traffic but will have no real impact on your business.

Check server response codes

Some SEO steps you can take to help your website are technical. One of these is server response codes to search robot requests. The wrong one can definitely affect your SEO.

1 Go to: http://responsetester.appspot.com/.

2 Input the URL of your home page on the search field there.

3 Click on the Test now! button.

We dwarves are natural sprinters. Very dangerous over short distances...

Contact Portent →

The Responsinator

Check for correct server response codes.

Enter your web site URL:

http://helpmyseo.com **2**

[Test now!] **3**

This is a tool created by Portent.

? DID YOU KNOW?
An improperly configured server can result in as much as a ten-place drop in the Google search rankings.

▶ SEE ALSO: Increase how quickly your website loads, in Chapter 1.

Increase conversions on your website

The success of your online business will depend upon your website's ability to convert casual visitors to paying customers. This is called the conversion rate and there are things you can do to improve it.

1 Have a newsletter subscription which allows site visitors to subscribe to your website and receive regular updates from you.

2 Make it easy to subscribe. Do not ask for too many details. Every field your visitors have to fill in halves the number who will actually do it.

3 Offer an alternative way for your online visitors to subscribe to your website's updates.

? DID YOU KNOW?
A newsletter can increase conversions from online visitors to customers by a factor as high as 25%.

HOT TIP: A newsletter is classed as a conversion form or a call to action. Calls to action help your online visitors decide how they want to access your services and improve the overall end-user experience to your website.

Identify seasonal peaks in your web traffic

When you understand the seasonal peaks and troughs of your website traffic you can best prepare your website by creating content specifically intended to attract visitors. Your best tool in this task is Google Analytics.

1 Go to your Google Analytics account (www.google.com/analytics) and log in using your Google email and password.

2 Select a suitably long date range to examine and make sure you are looking at daily traffic figures.

3 Check to see the top of the range.

4 Check your peaks and troughs in traffic.

Visitors Overview	Aug 1, 2011 - Jan 31, 2012
Advanced Segments Email BETA Export ▾ Add to Dashboard	

100.00% of total visits

Overview

Visits ▾ vs. Select a metric   Hourly **Day** Week Month

● Visits
1,000

3

500 **2**   **4**

? DID YOU KNOW?

When you boost the peaks and troughs in your annual traffic through the creation of content or even promotional offers which can attract more visitors, you can increase your website's ranking in search through increased Click Through Rate (CTR) scores.

HOT TIP: When you are trying to increase the volume of traffic during seasonal peaks you need to think about creating more than just your regular content. Competitions, special offers and time-limited events help focus potential customer attention and deliver targeted traffic to your website.

6 Analysing SEO performance

Introduction

You need to know how to analyse the SEO performance of your business in order to determine where to pour your energy, time and attention.

Mine SEO data from Google

Google Analytics is a powerful SEO tool which draws data directly from Google's Index. If the code is not already on your website you can see how to set it up here: http://goo.gl/EqHTW.

Go to your Google Analytics account and log in. Your dashboard gives you the following:

1 Number of daily visits.

2 Average time a visitor spends on your site.

3 Goal conversion rate (if you have set up Goals).

4 A break-down of how visitors get to your website.

5 A break-down of the country they come from.

DID YOU KNOW?
The visitor numbers reported by Google Analytics are an approximation. There is a small percentage of error due to a rounding down of figures. The actual number may be a little higher.

HOT TIP: Goals set up on your website allow you to assign a monetary value to each visitor who reaches that stage and therefore track the worth of your traffic in sterling figures.

Use Real-Time Analytics

Google Analytics now allows you to start a social media marketing campaign, where you share your website content and track activity and visitor numbers in real time.

1 In Google Analytics click on Real Time Beta and then Overview.

2 See instant visitor numbers in real time and their break-down.

3 See pages served per minute.

4 Analyse which URLs have brought your visitors to your website.

5 See which geographic location they came from.

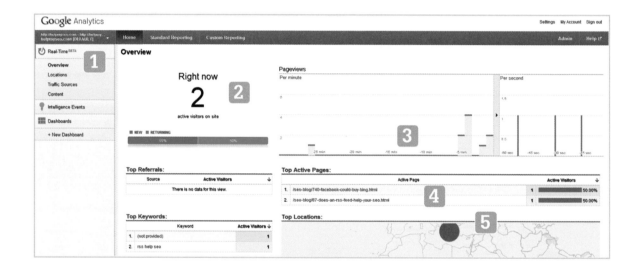

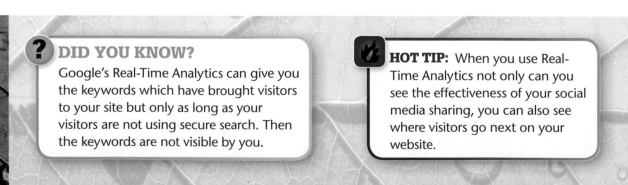

? DID YOU KNOW?
Google's Real-Time Analytics can give you the keywords which have brought visitors to your site but only as long as your visitors are not using secure search. Then the keywords are not visible by you.

HOT TIP: When you use Real-Time Analytics not only can you see the effectiveness of your social media sharing, you can also see where visitors go next on your website.

Use visualisation to see where visitors go on your website

Use data visualisation to help you understand how your website is used and how it can be improved.

1. Go to the Standard Reporting tab.

2. Click on Audience>Visitors Flow.

3. A slider allows you to expand the visitor flow for easier analysis.

4. See where your site visitors stop.

5. See what percentage gets through to the landing pages you need them to and what the drop-off rate is.

? DID YOU KNOW?
Visitors who have more than one interaction on your website (i.e. get to more than one page) are 40% more likely to convert into paying customers.

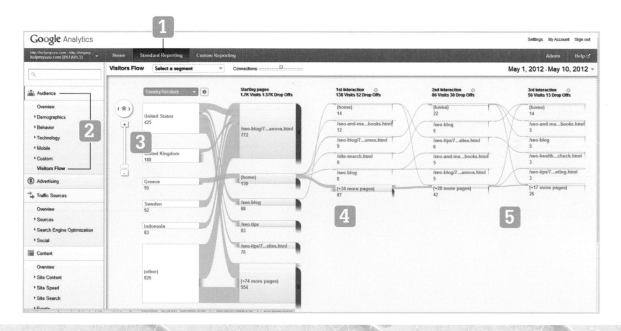

HOT TIP: Visualising the visitor flow on your website enables you to see where visitors go and you can then place a call to action on those pages in order to take advantage of the traffic.

ALERT: If you see that only a small percentage of visitors gets to your conversion pages, you need to work harder on your website's calls to action (by perhaps increasing their number).

Understand how visitors find your website

Understand the different ways through which visitors come to your website and you have a ready-made blueprint to help you create an effective content marketing strategy.

1 See how traffic is broken down by percentage over a given period.

2 See the keywords which brought visitors to your website.

3 See the percentage of visits per keyword and analyse sources which brought you traffic.

6,832 people visited this site

- **48.32% Search Traffic**
  3,301 Visits
- **26.21% Referral Traffic**
  1,791 Visits
- **20.48% Direct Traffic**
  1,399 Visits
- **4.99% Campaigns**
  341 Visits

Search Traffic		Source	Visits	% Visits
Keyword	1.	stumbleupon.com	457	25.52%
Matched Search Query	2.	plus.url.google.com	405	22.61%
Source	3.	t.co	176	9.83%
Referral Traffic	4.	facebook.com	103	5.75%
Source	5.	socialmediatoday.com	91	5.08%
Direct Traffic	6.	inbound.org	55	3.07%
Landing Page	7.	diynot.com	51	2.85%
	8.	technorati.com	49	2.74%
	9.	merveozturkcan.com	41	2.29%
	10.	serpiq.com	34	1.90%

view full report

This report was generated on 5/11/12 at 12:04:38 AM - Refresh Report

? DID YOU KNOW?

Almost 50% of all traffic to websites comes from social media networks. It is important to identify which ones are responsible for the traffic which comes to your website.

Use Webmaster Tools to check your indexing

Google's Webmaster Tools has functionality which allows you to check whether your website has been indexed properly and if there are any additional issues you need to be aware of. The Dashboard on Webmaster Tools is a critical part of how you check your website.

1 Crawl Errors show you immediate issues in the indexing of your website.

2 URL Errors indicate pages of your website which cannot be found and whether there is any odd server behaviour.

3 See the number of times your website appeared on Google Search and the number of clicks it got.

4 Check to see the number of URLs your website has and the number which have actually been indexed.

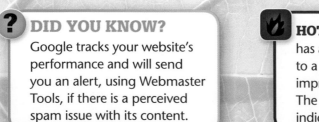

? DID YOU KNOW?
Google tracks your website's performance and will send you an alert, using Webmaster Tools, if there is a perceived spam issue with its content.

HOT TIP: The number of times your website has appeared on Google Search in response to a query is reflected in the number of impressions reported in Webmaster Tools. The increase or decrease of this number is an indication of your website's quality.

Use online tools to analyse your website

The on-page optimisation of your website plays a part in the way it is assessed by search engines in terms of quality. There are some handy online tools which allow you to check just how well it has been optimised.

1 Go to: http://goo.gl/vRRh.

2 Input the URL of your website there.

3 Use the number code to authenticate your entry.

4 Press Submit.

? DID YOU KNOW?
The meta tags of your website do not directly impact upon its SEO status but they do affect it indirectly. They are the ones a visitor first sees on the search engine results page which will convince them to click on that result.

HOT TIP: The loading time of your web page is also a criterion used by Google to ascertain its quality. This impacts on its search ranking.

ALERT: When placing your keywords be careful to not repeat any of them and keep them within a maximum of 12. Repeating keywords usually results in a Google penalty.

Spot poorly performing website pages

A poorly performing website page can affect your entire website. Spotting them and weeding them out is crucial for your website's search engine ranking.

1 Go to Google Analytics>Content>Overview.

2 Check highest page views per page.

3 Look at lowest page views per page.

HOT TIP: You are looking for highs and lows. Low-performing pages which give you few page views and high bounce rates need to be either weeded out or changed.

Page Title	Pageviews	% Pageviews
1. Social Media's Challenging Face		
May 1, 2012 - May 14, 2012	1,152	33.46%
Apr 1, 2012 - Apr 14, 2012	0	0.00%
% Change	100.00%	100.00%
2. Help My SEO: Insights in SEO, Social Media & Marketing by best-selling author.		
May 1, 2012 - May 14, 2012	354	10.28%
Apr 1, 2012 - Apr 14, 2012	414	9.34%
% Change	-14.49%	10.09%
3. Google Penguin Update Hits eCommerce Websites		
May 1, 2012 - May 14, 2012	121	3.51%
Apr 1, 2012 - Apr 14, 2012	0	0.00%
% Change	100.00%	100.00%
4. Google Penguin Update SEO Health Check		
May 1, 2012 - May 14, 2012	82	2.38%
Apr 1, 2012 - Apr 14, 2012	0	0.00%
% Change	100.00%	100.00%
5. The Social Media Mind		
May 1, 2012 - May 14, 2012	75	2.18%
Apr 1, 2012 - Apr 14, 2012	21	0.47%
% Change	257.14%	359.84%
6. Harvard and M.I.T. are Disrupting Education with Free Online Courses		
May 1, 2012 - May 14, 2012	66	1.92%
Apr 1, 2012 - Apr 14, 2012	0	0.00%
% Change	100.00%	100.00%

WHAT DOES THIS MEAN?

Bounce rate: The number of people who abandon a certain page. A high bounce rate used to be a metric of poor quality in a website but now has become a relatively normal thing to expect as online visitors frequently read the content of one page and quickly move on.

Use the Google Panda update to boost your website

The Google Panda update is an update in the Google search algorithm designed to help websites which have high-quality content get the traffic they deserve. Help your website benefit from this algorithmic change through the following steps.

1 Use short, descriptive page titles to describe your content.

2 Use social media sharing buttons.

3 Use attractive illustrations to illustrate your content.

4 Use long form content of at least 450 words.

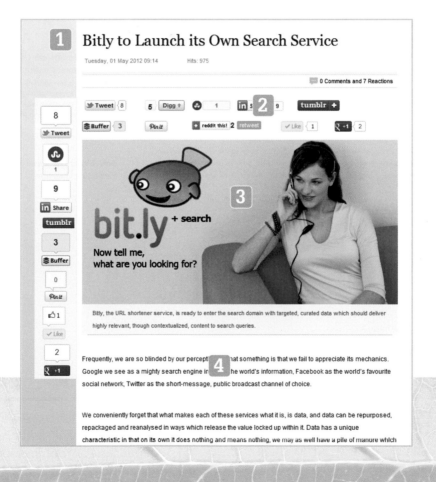

5 Use multimedia where possible to enhance your content.

The year that's about to close is probably going to be most noted for the number and depth of social media disasters we saw it give us. From Gilbert Gottfried losing his gig as the voice of the Aflac duck after posting jokes about the tsunami, in Japan, on his Twitter account to "Two and a Half Men" star Ashton Kutcher being rebuked after tweeting to the 8.5 million followers of his @aplusk account, "How do you fire Jo Pa?" there was a plethora of celebrities, personalities and brands getting it wrong, and doing so spectacularly and in public.

The video tells a story of almost unbelievable social media ineptitude. It'll take just 10 minutes of your time and you will be astounded at some of the mistakes made:

5

42
🐦 Tweet
♻
5
33
in Share
tumblr
1
⬆ Buffer
0
📌 Pin it
👍 27
f Like
5
🔍 +1

**David Amerland's picks:
The Top T ▶ cial Media
Disasters of 2011**

🔊 0:00 YouTube

There were so many picks to choose form that to get to a shortlist of ten for this year's Top Ten Social Media Disasters, I had to sort through no fewer than 35 different case files and choose the ones which were the groundbreakers. Groundbreakers, by definition reach a milestone of sorts and provide us with a lesson that's hard to forget.

Each of the ten cases you get to hear about in the short video I compiled shows, to some extent similar symptoms of a lack of understanding of how social media truly works. When you get so many brands and so many different companies getting it wrong in so many different fields it is a clear indication that this is not just a

Social Media Meltdown: The Brian Presley and Melissa Stetten Story

11-06-2012 Hits:1598 **WEB View**

You May Also Like

Google Paid Ads Become More Compelling

I have never been a great fan of paid advertising. It's a hang up from my days when I worked on the coalface of SEO and clients had to be weaned from their overt reliance on PPC campaigns to gain...

21-02-2012 Hits:977 **Google News**

Google's Dominance Of The Web Search Market Continues To Grow

When it comes to dominating the search engine world there are two figures that matter and they are both important. One is the number of search queries which each search engine gets and they are growing for ...

14-04-2011 Hits:1358 **SEO Tips**

Search And The Social Media Marketing Question

? DID YOU KNOW?
Attractive illustrations which have been optimised properly help increase traffic to a website page and keep visitors there longer.

🔥 HOT TIP: When there is multimedia content on a page, in the form of podcasts or YouTube videos, it increases the likelihood of social network re-sharing.

Measure the marketing grade of your website

The marketing grade of your website is also a measure of its quality and the authority it can achieve on the Web against similar websites. It is comprised of many different factors and it is algorithmically calculated.

1 Go to http://marketing.grader.com and input your website's home page URL.

2 Check out your website's overall score out of 100.

3 See what percentage you get in the different sections of your website for which you are graded.

4 Go further down and follow the rest of the recommendations made by the report.

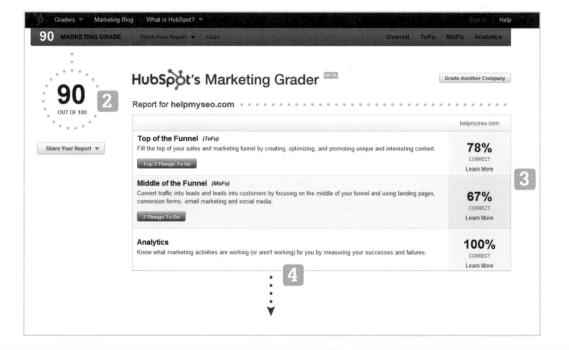

HOT TIP: A call to action or a conversion form on the most popular landing pages of your website will increase the number of conversions you get from visitors to potential customers.

Optimise your website images for better SEO

The speed at which your website loads is one of the ranking factors which Google uses to determine where it should appear in search. You can use professional photo-editing software like Photoshop to help optimise your website images, but you could also use a free online service.

1 Go to http://tools.dynamicdrive.com/imageoptimizer/.

2 Input in the field the URL of a website image (or upload one from your computer).

3 Choose the type of file you want to change the image to (or select to keep it the same).

4 Choose optimize to see the results.

DID YOU KNOW?

Optimised images can significantly speed up your website's loading speed, particularly when your website is getting a lot of traffic.

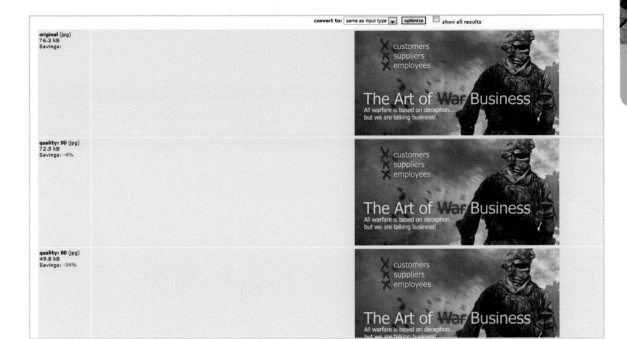

HOT TIP: Tick the show all results box in the online picture optimiser tool to see exactly what the quality of the image will be at different levels of compression and optimisation.

ALERT: Be careful, when reducing the file size of images, to not degrade pictures to the point where they stop working on the visual appeal of your website. Although a fast-loading site is desirable, there is a trade-off between a site that loads really quickly and a website which cannot keep its visitors because of poor-quality images.

7 Commenting systems and SEO

Introduction

When you implement a commenting system on your website you leverage user-generated content to help augment your website's keywords and further help its SEO in ways which you could not do using normal text content.

Learn how user-generated content helps your website

When you create content on your website you encounter two small but important issues. First, you cannot always accurately predict the keywords which would be used by those searching for your website. Second, you cannot repeat, too many times, the main keywords you want to rank for without running the risk of incurring an SEO penalty.

1 Specific keywords have been used in the title of this article.

2 They have been further enhanced in the caption of the picture which illustrates it.

3 They are reinforced by the copy in the main article body

DID YOU KNOW?

Comments are indexed by Google and can appear higher on Google search for comment-specific search terms than the piece itself.

HOT TIP: A commenting system allows the creation of further content on your website long after you have finished writing a particular article and moved on.

Choose a commenting system for your website

There are several commenting systems you can use. Some are native to website programming and others need to be installed. The latter have a distinct advantage over the former as they allow you to tap into their own already created communities and give you the possibility of attracting even more traffic that way.

- Specific login allows you to create a profile and become a member of the existing community.

- Log in using any existing social network login.

- Disqus community members themselves can see comments and topics and get to your website.

? DID YOU KNOW?

Commenting systems offer several different ways of controlling spam and moderating comments, placing you in total control of what is added to your website.

HOT TIP: A commenting system acts like an interlinked messaging system within the commenting system community. This has the power to start off and enhance conversations between commenting system community members, which take place right on your website.

Choose an alternative commenting system

The importance of a commenting system to your SEO is such that you should never take it lightly. Disqus, in the section before, is one viable choice. Another one is offered by Livefyre.

1 Livefyre comments allow you to own the data which means that comments are written in the database of your website.

2 There is an easy installation process and integration with social media platforms.

3 Livefyre is compatible with many popular content management system platforms.

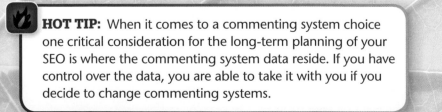

HOT TIP: When it comes to a commenting system choice one critical consideration for the long-term planning of your SEO is where the commenting system data reside. If you have control over the data, you are able to take it with you if you decide to change commenting systems.

Explore Our Features

See Our Products

Get Social | Blazing Real-Time | Activate Community | Moderate with Ease | StreamHub

2

Tagging

Now your community can invite their Facebook and Twitter friends to engage with your content right from the comment box. Give your readers access to their entire social network to bring specific friends to the conversation.

joebertino

I love this post. Check it out @JMattHicks @jenna

Your Twitter and Facebook friends

jennalanger

Jenna Langer

jenna (jenna)

New Account »   or sign in with

Facebook   twitter

Google   Linked in

Log In   OpenID

Powered by Janrain

Sign In

Make it simple for readers to join your community. Users have the option to sign in with multiple social networks to put a face to their name and comments.

HOT TIP: There are rumours in the SEO industry that some time soon Google is going to unveil a Google commenting system. Unless there is an urgent need for you to integrate a commenting system on your website now, waiting a couple of months will pay off handsomely in terms of SEO impact and comments.

DID YOU KNOW?
Comments do not subscribe to the same restrictions as content in article posts and web pages. You can include keywords there with greater emphasis than you would on a web page.

Use commenting to help your SEO

The comments on your website should be part of your SEO strategy and help your website increase its keyword range without appearing to try unnaturally hard in terms of how these keywords are placed there.

1 Commenters, responding to the original post, add extra value to it in terms of information.

2 The length of the original post, as data, is increased.

3 Keywords can be inserted in the reply and acknowledgement as necessary.

Showing 2 comments

Sort by popular now ▾

Kay Riley **1**

Great post!! With so many places one can go to look for a job, it does help to start with the bigger ones as you mentioned. Here's another article about using these social media sites for your job search: http://applicant.com/linkedin-...

I also find that with so many people on the go, they like to take their job hunting sites with them so they can read them between interviews or network meetings. Here's another article I thought present some options very well: http://www.cbsnews.com/8301-50... **2**

I also agree with you that having a presence online is essential to any job seeker who wants to stand out in the crowd. With so many places for prospective employees to look, I would suggest one's personal branding blog be titled and Search Engine friendly so those in their desired industry will be able to find them.

2 days ago   2 Likes   Like Reply

David Amerland, Author of books on SEO and Social Media Marketing **3** -optimist.

Kay, thank you for your contribution here. The additional info you have added (and links) do a great job of adding depth to the article and, as you suggest, using social media to get a job is only increasing.

7 hours ago   in reply to Kay Riley   Like Reply

HOT TIP: You can create interaction in your website posts by ending them in a way which invites it, either because the conclusion is controversial or because the subject matter is.

? DID YOU KNOW?

Comments made through a commenting system are visible to the online community of users the commenting system has. This creates a certain amount of curiosity and brings more visitors to your website.

WHAT DOES THIS MEAN?

Comment bait: Content on your website which is written to invite interaction. Also called comment fodder.

Benefit from a commenting system

User-generated content, which is what comments on your website are, is hard to come by. Online visitors have little time and even less inclination to comment publicly. This means that you need to help them do so through the type of content you post.

1 Use subject matter and titles with broad appeal to invite opinion as opposed to expertise.

2 Socialise the content widely in order to attract attention.

3 Comments add depth and interactivity to your content.

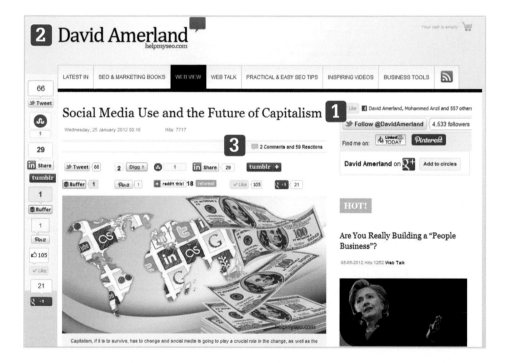

? DID YOU KNOW?
Comments added to a page on your website count towards the overall length of the original post. This adds value to the page in the eyes of a search engine and helps rank it higher.

🔥 HOT TIP: Use a news service such as Google News (http://news.google.com) to help you stay abreast of breaking news across the Web which you may be able to use in your marketing.

Showing 2 comments

Sort by popular now

Meg Tufano

Wow, David, I really learned a lot! I only have helped one company with anything that would be related to what you describe in your wonderfully rich "countdown." I was asked to help a company decide essentially how to organize their company which planned to do about twenty different services. The owner was "all over the place" (apparently a common reality (;')) and I listened to her ideas as long as I could, read everything she had and then did what ANYONE with half a brain would do: I made sure her choice of name was a domain that was open.

Well, you know the answer.

I gave her a good structure for what she wanted to do, figuring out the logical ways her twenty services could fit into three areas (almost all having to do with Washington, D.C. real estate, the value of which is always increasing in value so they really DO live in a bubble). I gave her storyboard-type of presentation (I never use Powerpoint if I can help it); and a nice handful of Photoshopped original photographs that would work well on her web site related to the services.

She was excited and happy with the results, especially because she could get her own head around what she wanted to do. But her partner went crazy at the name change and dropped out of the whole thing. Essentially, angry because she hadn't done the first, obvious, thing the year or so BEFORE they bought stationery and all the old-school stuff.

I learned more than they did! But they paid their bill on time and gave me some referrals, so all-in-all, not a bad experience (except that their company never got off the ground and—I cannot help it—I really only enjoy doing things that help people get where they want to go). They are both in real estate now and making big bucks selling houses (like falling off a log in DC), so? I guess I shouldn't worry about them!

Pleasure meeting you today. Your writing shows that you know whereof you speak, always a nice confirmation of a first impression.

I assume you've read Soros' "The Capitalist Threat" http://www.mtholyoke.edu/acad/...

And the conservative Krum's article on how the liberal Krugman may be right: http://articles.businessinside...

I have about five books that are "what I know" about online everything:

Clark, Ruth (2003) Building expertise. Washington D.C.: International Society for Performance Improvement.

http://www.amazon.com/Building...

[Amazon] This third edition of the classic resource, Building Expertise draws on the most recent evidence on how to build innovative forms of expertise and translates that evidence into guidelines for instructional designers, course developers and facilitators, technical communicators, and other human performance professionals. Ruth Colvin Clark summarizes psychological theories concerning ways instructional methods support human learning processes. Filled with updated research and new illustrative examples, this new edition offers trainers evidence-based guidelines to help them accelerate genuine expertise within their organizations.

HOT TIP: Successfully news-jack a breaking story by finding a way to mirror its title in the headline of the content you produce for your website.

WHAT DOES THIS MEAN?

News jacking: The technique of using breaking news to help find angles which then promote your website and its content.

Create a commenting system policy

Commenting takes time, effort and some thought. Site visitors who have commented have been touched, in some way, by the content on your website. You need to have a commenting policy in place so you know how to best respond to them.

1 Create titles that fit in with your overall approach to the online conversation.

2 Check popularity of the article through its social sharing appeal.

3 Check to see comments and responses to your post.

? DID YOU KNOW?
Commenting on website content frequently helps add greater value to the original content by asking questions and adding points which have not been covered yet.

🔥 HOT TIP: Respond to comments quickly. Studies show that fast responses lead to better engagement and invite further comments and social sharing of the content.

WHAT DOES THIS MEAN?
Comment hook: Commenting in a way which helps not just answer the question or respond to the comment but also create the opportunity for further engagement and interaction.

Develop a successful comment-creation strategy

The secret to creating the kind of content which helps generate reactions and comments and helps your website get noticed lies in having a helpful content strategy in place.

1 Go to http://news.yahoo.com/blogs/trending-now/.

2 Pick content which is trending across the Web and fits in with your website's subject matter.

3 Think carefully about how you are going to integrate that content in your website through writing new material.

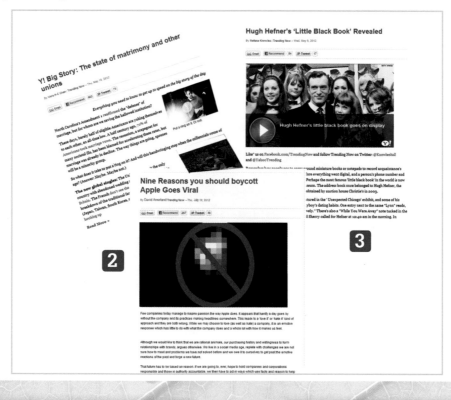

HOT TIP: Create great content which attracts comments by being opportunistic. Do not force it. The moment you find the content you need which fits in with what you do, go for it.

HOT TIP: Help attract attention to your content by sharing it across social networks as much as possible. Exposure leads to interaction, which helps add commenters and comments to your post.

Measure engagement

Engagement is a crucial element of your content marketing and its impact on the SEO of your website. Content which gets commented on and re-shared rises higher in the search algorithm and helps your website's visibility.

1 The social activity of the content you create is one clear signal of engagement.

2 The comments which are made in response to the content are also a signal of engagement.

3 Commenters who come back to your website and reply to your reply are a strong signal of engagement.

HOT TIP: Engage your audience in each social network by using the social network buttons on your website (Google Plus, Facebook, Twitter).

? DID YOU KNOW?
Every social network has its own way of connecting within it. Twitter is a broadcast machine, Facebook is where you connect with your friends (and ask for their help to spread your content) and Google Plus is where you find people of similar interests.

WHAT DOES THIS MEAN?
Engagement metrics: The term given to whatever means you use to measure engagement in each network. In Google Plus it will be +1s, in Facebook Likes and in Twitter re-Tweets.

8 Social media and SEO

Introduction

Search engine optimisation without a strong social media component will give you only half the ability you are looking for to help promote your website in Google's search results pages.

Learn how social media affects your website's SEO

Your website's presence in a social media environment affects its SEO because the way its content is shared and re-shared and commented upon is part of what Google considers to be your website's 'social signal'.

1 A large number of re-shares in Twitter brings traffic but also draws the attention of search engines.

2 LinkedIn re-shares aid the process.

3 Facebook Likes also lead to the kind of traffic that Google notices.

4 The number of people who come to a single page from such exposure far outweighs those from other website pages which have not experienced the same degree of social media success.

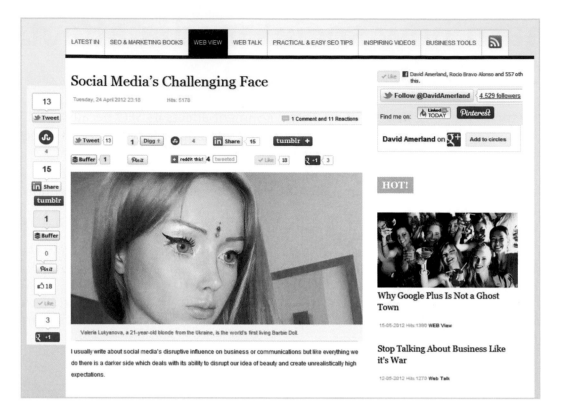

WHAT DOES THIS MEAN?

Social signal: The term Google applies to the social activity which takes place through a website's content. This includes initial sharing in social media networks and the engagement which follows once a link is posted there.

DID YOU KNOW?

Google Plus, Google's own social network, is now part of the metrics Google uses to assess and correctly rank a website. If your website's content is not being shared there it is unlikely to do very well.

ALERT:

Google has an 'Over-SEO Filter' which looks for websites which always share their content in a specific pattern. Google marks this as artificial and adjusts a website's ranking accordingly.

Use social media marketing to help your SEO

Market the content of your website through social media networks and you will begin to see an increase in traffic to your website as well as an improvement in your search result pages ranking.

1 Share your content on a social media network (such as Google Plus).

2 Create a catchy description to attract social network engagement.

3 Get comments and reactions to increase the value of the link you have posted in the eyes of a search engine. It will then be quickly indexed by Google and placed high.

LATEST IN   SEO & MARKETING BOOKS   WEB VIEW   WEB TALK   PRACTICAL & EASY SEO TIPS   INSPIRING VIDEOS   BUSINESS TOOLS

How can a Business Develop a Conscience?

Saturday, 19 May 2012 17:58   Hits: 368

✓ Like ▢ David Amerland, Mohammed Anzil and 557 others

▶ Follow @DavidAmerland 4,530 followers

Find me on: LinkedIn TODAY   Pinterest

David Amerland on g+   Add to circles

💬 0 Comments and 6 Reactions

🐦 Tweet 6   0   Digg +   ♨ 1   in Share 7   tumblr +

⬆ Buffer 1   Pin it   + reddit this! 0   tweet   ✓ Like 7   g+1 2

This is a week where I get to ask some hard questions and one of them is just how does a conscience manifest itself in a business model. After all any business is set up to do one thing well, and that is to m... money. We could argue that success in this field justifies the reason the business has been set... all is well. Whatever it is that the business had to do in order to become successful can be e... forgiven and perhaps, even, forgotten.

That approach however opens the door to all sorts of improprieties. And the problem... business operates in a vacuum. What it does and how it does it affects the commu... that community is situated within. And depending on the scale of the damage it ha... create a snowball effect where the adverse impact of any action is greatly magnifie... large. Small problems then become large ones very quickly. Technical issues bec... solutions which were intended to handle a business-related issue, no longer work...

In this *Online Marketing Help* podcast we look at just how a business can be made to de... Best-selling SEO and Social Media Marketing author, David Amerland, explains.

How Can a Business Develop a Conscience? by David Amerland ▾ Download

...a Business Develop a Conscience?

About 1,710,000 results (0.26 seconds)

erything
Images
Maps
Videos
News
Shopping
More

how search tools

How can a Business Develop a Conscience?
helpmyseo.com/.../759-how-can-a-business-develop-a-cons...
David Amerland - in 4,745 Google+ circles · More by David Amerland
1 day ago – This is a week where I get to ask some hard questions and one of them is just how does a **conscience** manifest in a **business** model.

How do we develop a conscience? - Yahoo! Answers
answers.yahoo.com › ... › Social Science › Psychology - Cached
3 answers - 17 Nov 2008
There is a lot of controversy on how the **conscience develops** but most research **does** agree on these fundamentals. 1. Moral sensitivity - The ...

CSR: Has big business developed a conscience?
www.arabiansupplychain.com/...business-developed-a-consci... - Cached
4 Dec 2011 – Home / CSR: Has big **business developed a conscience**? ... Corporate social responsibility is a complex field which **can** take on a multitude of different ...

CSR: Has big business developed a conscience ...
www.arabiansupplychain.com/...business-developed-a-consci... - Cached
4 Dec 2011 – Home / CSR: Has big **business developed a conscience**? ... Whilst ...'s CSR strategy **could** more typically be deemed as a community based

🔥 **HOT TIP:** Google Plus is Google's own social network and is quickly indexed by its search engine bot. Content placed there is in the Google Index within a day.

❓ **DID YOU KNOW?** When you place content in the Google Plus social network it is assessed against the social signal which your website and Google Profile generate and this leads to an assessment of your online authority.

Market your website's content using social media

Market your website's content in a social media environment by creating a 'voice' for the content you share which accurately reflects the character of your business and the way it works.

1. Choose the content which you are going to share.

2. Decide what your message will be when you share it.

3. Decide who you are going to share it with.

4. Be prepared to respond to comments and reactions.

DID YOU KNOW?

The tone and style you use to communicate your messages in a social media network setting create the 'voice' of your business and help customers identify who you are and what you do.

Hide comments ✕

[face image] ██████ ███████ May 15, 2012 [+1] - Reply
██████ ████ ███ ████████ ███ ██ ███ ████████ █████ █████ ██ ████

David Amerland May 15, 2012 Edit
+Heidi Schabziger exactly. It was easy to forget this with search and Google because to a certain degree the logic-rules which govern search can be gamed.

JJ Currie May 15, 2012 [+1] - Reply
Good old fashion marketing principles are coming to the fore online... We need to focus on providing quality content that benefits the user and adds value to the web.

David Amerland May 15, 2012 Edit
+JJ Currie Absolutely! This is what Google has wanted us to do all along. Many webmasters and marketers get sucked in the chase of search engines with the type of results we see today with the Penguin update.

JJ Currie May 15, 2012 [+1] - Reply
+David Amerland Agreed I think it became too easy to game the SERPS and most webmasters lost track of who they were trying to connect with...

David Amerland May 15, 2012 Edit +1
You are absolutely right! Semantic search is just round the corner so it is good to see a return to some kind of sanity in terms of online marketing. It should also help separate the wheat from the chaff, so to speak. Marketing without substance will finally drop off the charts irrespective of the quality of technical SEO and link-building done. This is a win-win for decent marketers, good businesses and, obviously, consumers.

JJ Currie May 15, 2012 [+1] - Reply
+David Amerland Hell Yeah!

🔥 **HOT TIP:** Create a message which you want to get across by putting together a collection of content you want to share which supports it. Reinforce that message by adding just the right tone of additional commentary.

🔥 **HOT TIP:** Share content on a social network at a time when you can monitor the responses and respond to them. This leads to further engagement and interaction, which helps your social signal and adds to the quality of your SEO.

Choose the channels for marketing your website

Social media marketing is time intensive. Its requirement that you devote at least some time in generating interaction and responding to it presents a challenge many businesses struggle to overcome. Your choice of network is important.

1 Google Plus is a social network which helps you connect with potential customers across the globe.

2 Twitter allows you to make use of the real-time Web to connect with potential customers on time-sensitive issues.

3 Facebook connects you to friends and contacts from the real world.

! ALERT: Post content from your website to social networks but only after the additional, explanatory text and its tone have been carefully worked out as it creates the context of your social network contact and helps create your online persona.

? DID YOU KNOW?
Research statistics show that Twitter is the best social platform possible for developing a brand and increasing brand recognition.

HOT TIP: Save time by linking up your Facebook account to Twitter by following the instructions on http://goo.gl/NqGke. The 140-character limit of Twitter is more forgiving than any of the other social networks, which require a lot more time and attention.

Use social media keyboard shortcuts

Use keyboard shortcuts in your social media marketing when you are short of time or need to get some things done quickly. The accumulated time saved over fairly simple executional tasks translates to a little more time to devote to your business and marketing.

1 Each web browser responds to the same set of keyboard shortcuts.

2 Each social network has its own set of keyboard shortcuts.

3 Using keyboard shortcuts helps prevent straining your wrist but, more importantly, saves precious time.

Google Chrome	Mozilla Firefox	Facebook
Alt M 1	Shift Alt M	New Message
Alt 0	Shift Alt 0	Help Center
Alt 1	Shift Alt 1	Home Page
Alt 2	Shift Alt 2	Profile Page
Alt 3	Shift Alt 3	Manage Friend List
Alt 4	Shift Alt 4	Messages List
Alt 5	Shift Alt 5	Notification Page
Alt 6	Shift Alt 6	Account Settings
Alt 7	Shift Alt 7	Privacy Settings
Alt 8	Shift Alt 8	Facebook Fan Page
Alt 9	Shift Alt 9	Facebook Terms
Alt ?	Shift Alt ?	Search Box

HOT TIP: Use keyboard shortcuts for even simple tasks on each social network to familiarise yourself with them.

Keyboard shortcuts

Actions
2

f : favorite
r : reply
t : retweet
m : direct message
n : new Tweet
enter : toggle details pane

Navigation

? : this menu
j : next Tweet
k : previous Tweet
space : page down
/ : search
. : refresh Tweets and back to top

Timelines

g h : home
g r : replies / mentions
g p : profile
g f : favorites
g m : messages
g u : go to user

Google+ Shortcut Keys

Key	Action
J	Scroll down to next Google+ stream update **3**
K	Scroll up to previous Google+ stream update
QQ	Pressing Q twice moves your cursor the search box in the "chat" section of Google+
Space	Scroll down stream by regular intervals
Space + Shift	Scroll up stream by regular intervals
Enter	When a stream update is selected Enter moves your cursor to the comment box
Enter + Tab	Submit comment
@	@ followed by a username is used to mention someone in a post or share the post with them

---

? **DID YOU KNOW?**

Time studies carried out by Google showed that over the course of a year the average social media network user who employs keyboard shortcuts can benefit by as much as nine extra hours.

Measure how effective your social media marketing is in Twitter

Marketing the content of your website in social media networks helps your SEO and its ranking in Google's search pages. You need to be able to measure just how effective your efforts are.

1 Go to www.tweetreach.com.

2 Input the search term you have been using to market your content in Twitter.

3 Click on the search icon.

4 Check out the results which show the reach of your messages in the Twitter network.

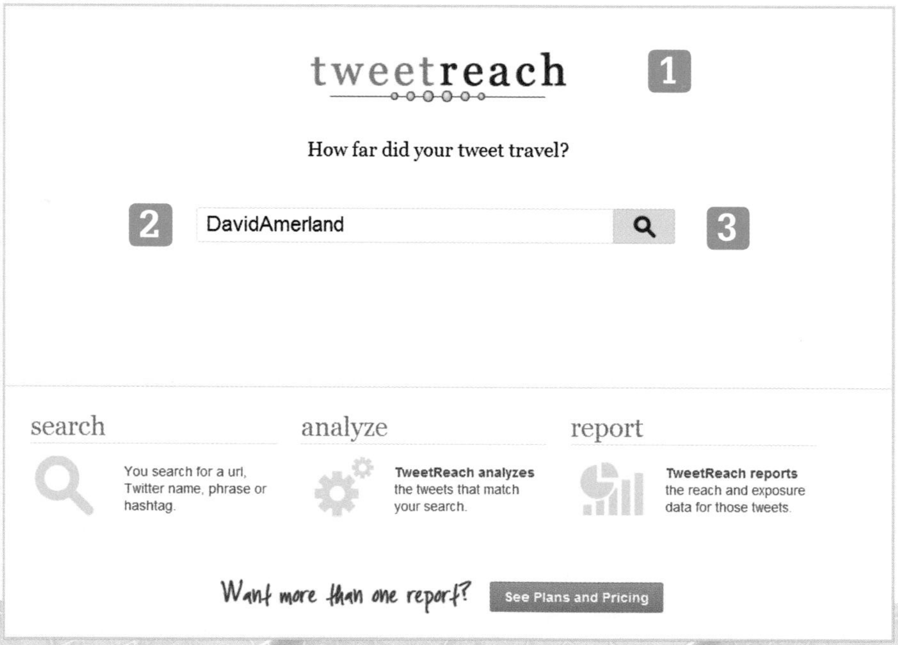

tweetreach

1

How far did your tweet travel?

2 DavidAmerland 🔍 **3**

search
🔍 You search for a url, Twitter name, phrase or hashtag.

analyze
⚙ **TweetReach analyzes** the tweets that match your search.

report
📊 **TweetReach reports** the reach and exposure data for those tweets.

Want more than one report? See Plans and Pricing

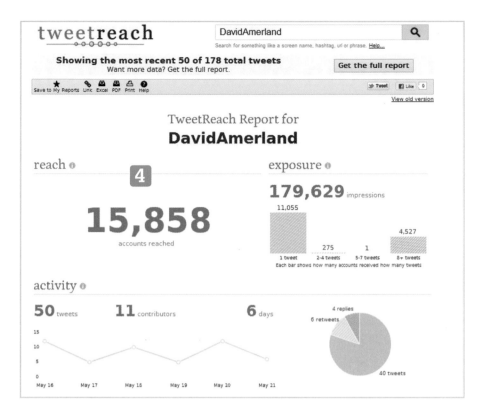

HOT TIP: Look in Tweetreach for your Twitter handle to best assess how far your messages travel and how many people they reach.

? DID YOU KNOW?
The messages you place in the Twitter social network will reach a different number of people depending on the time of day you post and the number of posts you have per day.

! ALERT: When it comes to marketing your business through Twitter you should know that a single Tweet can reach a maximum of 12% of your total number of followers. You will need to re-Tweet your messages strategically throughout the day.

Measure how effective your social media marketing is in Google Plus

See how effective your Google Plus marketing is by accurately measuring the reach of your posts in the Google Plus social network and the interaction they generate.

1 Go to www.circlecount.com.

2 Log in using your Google Plus profile.

3 Check to see the statistics on the interaction of your posts in the social network.

? DID YOU KNOW?
Google Plus is more than a social network. Google has turned it into an online identity service where the activity of your Google profile is monitored and assessed and becomes part of its social signal.

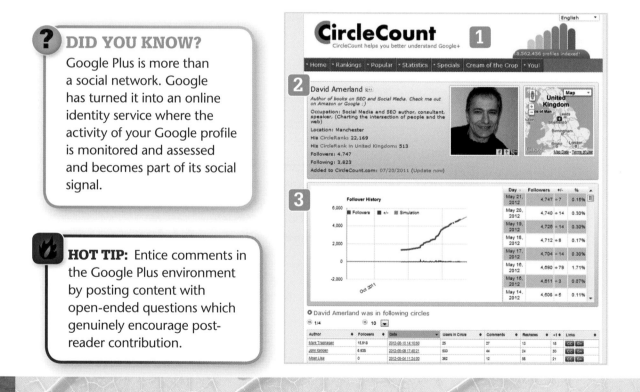

HOT TIP: Entice comments in the Google Plus environment by posting content with open-ended questions which genuinely encourage post-reader contribution.

WHAT DOES THIS MEAN?

Ripples: A graphic interface which shows immediately the number of times your content is shared on the Google Plus platform along with the number of people this has affected.

Use Twitter in your marketing campaign

Make Twitter a vital part of your campaign and use the power of the real-time Web to help both your SEO and your online marketing. Key to this is the structure of your Tweets.

1 Use a keyword hashtag when formulating your Tweet.

2 Shorten your URL using a URL shortener like www.bitly.com so you can track it.

3 Use a category hashtag so your Tweet comes up in Twitter search.

? DID YOU KNOW?

Use hashtags every time you want to make your Tweets come up on Twitter search which is by topic (such as #social) or category (#socialmedia).

HOT TIP: Monitor Twitter Trends (http://monitter.com/) and be prepared to find ones which directly apply to your business so that you can benefit from the attention they receive.

SEE ALSO: Chapter 7 and news jacking. The technique also applies to Twitter marketing with the hijacking of Twitter Trends to help raise the profile of your Tweets.

9 SEO and paid advertising

Introduction

Many factors can affect your website's SEO status. One of them is the amount of traffic your website gets. Google sees the traffic landing on your website and how it behaves and uses it to assess the quality of your website and its ranking. If you can get more people to visit your website you have the opportunity to make Google notice it more.

Learn what pay-per-click advertising is

Pay-per-click (PPC) is web advertising which costs you only when someone clicks on it to be taken to your website. Google is the largest global player in the PPC market with the Google AdWords program.

1 Go to: https://adwords.google.com/.

2 Familiarise yourself with the layout.

3 Check out the tools which are provided to help you track your results.

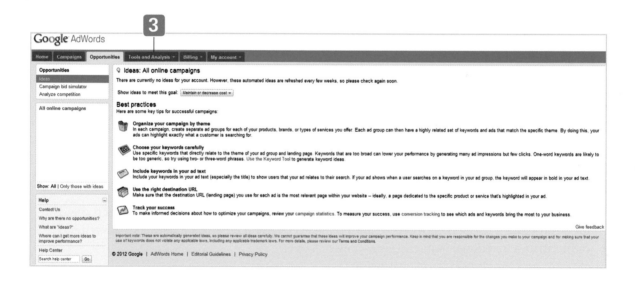

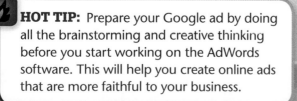

HOT TIP: Prepare your Google ad by doing all the brainstorming and creative thinking before you start working on the AdWords software. This will help you create online ads that are more faithful to your business.

4 Go to Campaigns to set up the advertising campaign for your website.

WHAT DOES THIS MEAN?

Pay-per-click (PPC): Also referred to in the online advertising business as CPC, which stands for cost-per-click. Google broke new ground in PPC by using an affiliate model of advertising rather than a traditional high-cost, low-presence one.

ALERT: You always need a budget to work successfully with Google AdWords. The AdWords interface lets you control your daily spend and the cost of each word for which your ad will appear. You will need to monitor this closely to see whether it is working the way you want it to.

Promote your website with keyword-specific Google ads

Use the power of Google AdWords to draw online visitors to your website based upon the same set of keywords for which you organically optimise your website.

1 Create short, punchy ad headlines which catch the visitor's eye.

2 Write enthusiastic descriptions which make people want to click.

3 Have a distinct, targeted set of keywords suited to your ad.

Ad preview

1 Get up-to minute updates
See the latest news from companies you care about. Sign up for Twitter
www.twitter.com

Ad preview 2

Get to know celebrities!
Sign up for Twitter and see what TV stars are up to in real life.
www.twitter.com

Enter one keyword per line. 3

Zappos
Jet Blue
Comcast
Starbucks
Southwest Airlines
Marriott
The Travel Channel

Enter one keyword per line.

Miley Cyrus
The Jonas Brothers
Zac Efron
Vanessa Hudgens
Ashley Tisdale
Drake Bell
Dylon Sprouse

? DID YOU KNOW?

Test your ad copy. Make several different ads. Target different types of keywords and tailor your ad language to your keywords. Let's say you were running an ad campaign for Twitter. Depending on your target audience, you'd want to vary the keywords and ad copy.

HOT TIP: Target your online audience by using keywords which tightly reflect the way they would search for what your business does. Separate your keywords into two or more groups with slightly different focus, create different ads for each and monitor to see which is best.

? DID YOU KNOW?

You can choose to target your Google AdWords to run on a PPC or you can go for a cost per thousand views (CPM) depending on the aims of your campaign and your budget.

Use the click-through rate (CTR) to maximise CPM

Use the CTR to determine your ads' performance. Adwords gives you statistics on how each keyword within each ad performed. This is particularly important when you're paying by CPM. You will want to make sure that one keyword isn't getting a ton of search hits but very few click-throughs.

1 In Google Adwords look at the number of clicks for each ad you create.

2 Look at the number of impressions.

3 See what the percentage rate is to determine the CTR.

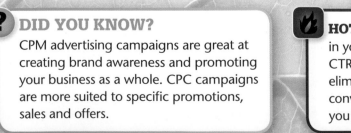

	1 Clicks	Impr.	CTR ⑦
		2	
Ad Copy 1	4	5,447	0.07%
Ad Copy 2	2	2,075	0.10% **3**

	Clicks	Impr.	CTR
Keyword 1	262	4,257	6.15%
Keyword 2	238	2,287	10.41%

? DID YOU KNOW?

CPM advertising campaigns are great at creating brand awareness and promoting your business as a whole. CPC campaigns are more suited to specific promotions, sales and offers.

🔥 HOT TIP: Achieve better results in your advertising by checking the CTR of the keywords in each ad and eliminating keywords which have low conversion rates but which still cost you money.

Use keywords to maximise CPC traffic to your website

The advantage of CPC is that you don't pay if Google users don't click. The disadvantage is that it tends to be more expensive if there's a decent CTR. So where the CPM buyer's goal is to find the areas where the CTR is highest, the CPC buyer's goal is to find the keywords that have the cheapest CPC.

1 Through the reporting tools in your Google Adwords account, check number of clicks per keyword.

2 Check the number of impressions and your CTR.

3 Check the cost per keyword for the clicks it received.

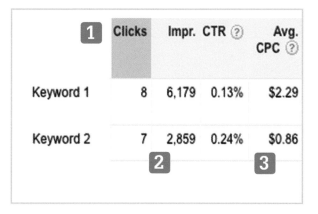

	1 Clicks	Impr.	CTR ⑦	Avg. CPC ⑦
Keyword 1	8	6,179	0.13%	$2.29
Keyword 2	7	2,859	0.24%	$0.86
		2		3

 DID YOU KNOW?

Once you've analysed all the data Google has collected, it's time to start making adjustments to your campaign. After all, what good is recognising that certain ads and keywords are underperforming if you don't remove them.

HOT TIP: If you aren't getting the number of clicks that you want, sometimes you'll have to pay a higher CPC or accept a lower CTR. This is why carrying out this analysis is important.

Learn how using paid advertising can help your SEO

Use paid advertising to drive more traffic to your website. This helps pick up the slack in slow times and it boosts your website's traffic signal at all times. The traffic your website gets is one of the factors Google uses to rank the site.

1 Identify the peaks in your monthly traffic.

2 Correlate those peaks with traffic from your online advertising.

3 Check your new to returning online visitor ratio.

4 Check your site statistics to determine just how 'sticky' your website is.

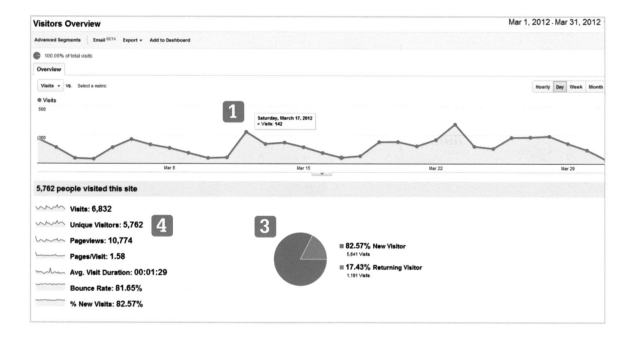

? DID YOU KNOW?

Google accumulates data on your website's activity and visitor behaviour, anonymously, and then uses it to make a value judgement on the quality of the end-user experience a website offers its visitors. The outcome of this judgement affects your ranking.

Learn to socialise your SEO

Use the power of social media to help your SEO further by leveraging your contacts and immediate online network of friends to boost your website content.

1 Use your Google Profile to log on to Google Plus.

2 Share your content in the public stream.

3 Use the Ripples tracking option to see the interaction in terms of re-shares to see how many it has reached.

HOT TIP: Increase interaction, comments and re-sharing by posting content which is interesting from an informational point of view and answers a crucial question your online audience may have, or by posting content that is fun to read.

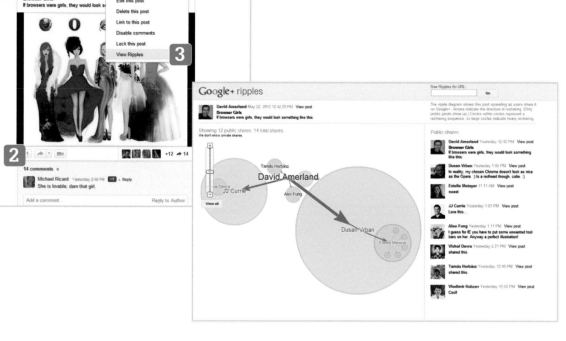

ALERT: Content that is fact-heavy in an overly assertive way discourages interaction and comments as those who read it feel that they are not expert enough to interact with it.

DID YOU KNOW?

Content that is interacted with and re-shared in the Google Plus network generates a social signal which Google uses to assess its importance in the search index. This directly affects your website's ranking.

Use paid traffic to increase time spent on your website

The longer website visitors stay on your website, the greater is the likelihood that they will then convert to paying customers. To keep them to your website you need to have a clever content strategy which helps increase engagement levels.

1 Have content that is intelligent, original and engaging.

2 Always suggest related content to help broaden the reader's horizons.

3 Have a 'hot content' feature to promote popular articles.

> **! ALERT:** Avoid turning off website visitors by presenting them with justified blocks of text or pages where there is nothing which helps break up the text and make it more accessible.

4 Have a slide-out feature which suggests at least one additional, related article.

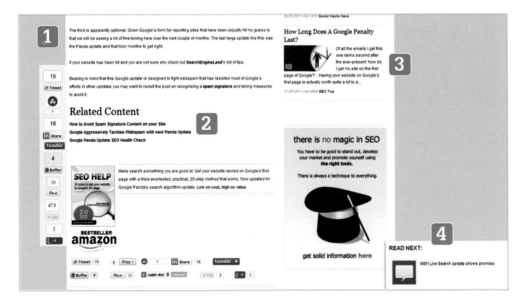

> **HOT TIP:** Liven up your content by breaking it up with graphics, pictures, subheadings and bullet points. They help make it more readable and easier for visitors to absorb.

> **? DID YOU KNOW?**
> Related content links and a slide-out feature help your online visitors find at least one more article to read on your website.

Create synergy between paid advertising and natural SEO

Paying for advertising on the Web is less effective when it does not help your website to stand out by also helping your organic search engine optimisation efforts. Bridging the two are your keywords.

1 Know which search queries deliver your website in organic search.

2 See where you rank.

3 Check to see what Google ads come up.

4 Adjust your keywords for peripheral search terms (such as 'SEO help' in the example) so your site comes up on Google Ads when keywords do not rank it in the organic search results page.

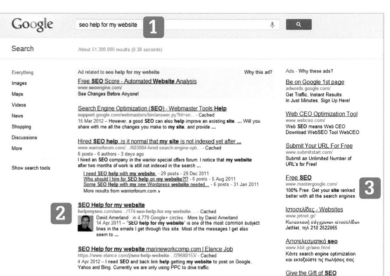

HOT TIP: Use your keyword research to create lists of words for which you rank organically and lists of peripheral words for which you do not. The latter should be used in your PPC campaign to help create a more constant presence of your website.

? DID YOU KNOW?
The traffic you get from paid advertising (PPC) contributes to the traffic figures you get naturally on your website and it is then used as one of the signals Google uses to assess your website's ranking on the organic search engine results pages.

? DID YOU KNOW?
The organic search engine results pages are collectively referred to as SERPs and a website's position in them is referred to as 'organic ranking in the SERPs'.

10 The real-time Web and SEO

Introduction

The real-time Web has become a priority tool for marketing as well as SEO. The presence of a website's content in the stream of the real-time Web sends a powerful signal to search engine bots, can help a website's ranking and helps it find new visitors to turn into customers.

Establish a real-time Web presence

There is only one real-time Web channel and that is Twitter. Facebook has recently changed its stream to be closer to Twitter's immediacy in terms of its refresh rate. There is a distinct SEO advantage in having a presence in both networks.

1 Have a Twitter profile which reflects your business or brand.

2 Populate your Twitter stream by following some people in your industry.

3 Tweet often about your specific topics.

? DID YOU KNOW?
Use Twitter to market time-sensitive content. The links included in Twitter's 140-character message are indexed by Google and become part of your website's social signal.

! ALERT: Use Twitter frequently throughout the day to reach as many of your followers as possible. Studies show that you can only hope to reach a maximum of 7–10% of your followers on a single Tweet so it is important to Tweet often.

🔥 HOT TIP: Twitter allows you to link it up to your Facebook profile and kill two birds with one stone by having your Tweets appear in your Facebook Timeline. This amplifies the reach of your Twitter marketing and social signal and helps your website's ranking in the SERPs.

Use the real-time Web to boost your website's rankings

Boost your website's rankings with a well-planned and executed real-time web marketing campaign which will refresh and amplify your website's social signal in Google's search engine.

1 Have a Tweeting schedule planned in advance.

2 Put together a good mix of social and promotional Tweets.

3 Stick to your schedule and marketing plan.

Twitter Tweeting Schedule

1

Monday
1. General hello
2. Business Tweet
3. Something from the news
4. Question to promote interaction
5. Link to blog

2

Tuesday
1. Link to news item
2. Video
3. Poll
4. Business Tweet
5. General personal comment

Wednesday
1. Business Tweet
2. Something from the news
3. Question
4. Link to blog
5. Welcome to new followers

Thursday
1. General hello
2. Request for help on something
3. Business Tweet
4. Connect on FB / LinkedIn
5. General comment

3

Friday
1. Follow Friday Tweets
2. Business Tweet
3. Question
4. Photograph
5. General comment

? DID YOU KNOW?
When you use Twitter the strength of your Tweet's social signal to Google Search fades within two hours or so. Tweets which are spaced apart to cover most of the day, amplify your social signal and help your website get noticed by Google Search.

HOT TIP: Repeat your Tweets a few hours apart and amplify the social signal content from your website sends to Google Search.

HOT TIP: Twitter's fast-moving stream makes it difficult to monitor what is being said about you and who is reacting to your posts. For that use a more user-friendly application like Bottlenose (http://bottlenose.com), which lets you monitor everything from one place.

Learn to interact on Twitter

Interact with those who respond to your Tweets on Twitter to increase engagement, gather more followers and have your posts seen by many more people. Bottlenose allows you to filter Twitter content in a more manageable way.

1 Monitor Mentions of yourself.

2 See who has shared your Tweets.

3 Respond to those who have engaged with your content.

4 Create as many filters as you need.

HOT TIP: Get into the habit of checking Twitter through the Bottlenose interface at least once a day so that you do not miss anything.

DID YOU KNOW?
Twitter's stream moves fast. Bottlenose allows you to go as far back as a week. So anything beyond that point which you have not responded to drops out of sight.

DID YOU KNOW?
When you link Twitter to your Facebook profile you increase the level of activity on both social networks and amplify the social signal your website sends out.

HOT TIP: Use Bottlenose to monitor LinkedIn and Facebook as well as Twitter. This helps you plan the impact of your Tweets much better.

Increase the authority of your website

Increase the authority of your website and you will see a corresponding increase in search ranking and organic traffic.

1 Start by creating content which is compelling enough to attract the attention of your target audience.

2 Make it easy for your target audience to re-share your content on social networks.

3 Content shared in social networks gains wider exposure.

4 It gets picked up by bloggers who then link back to your website.

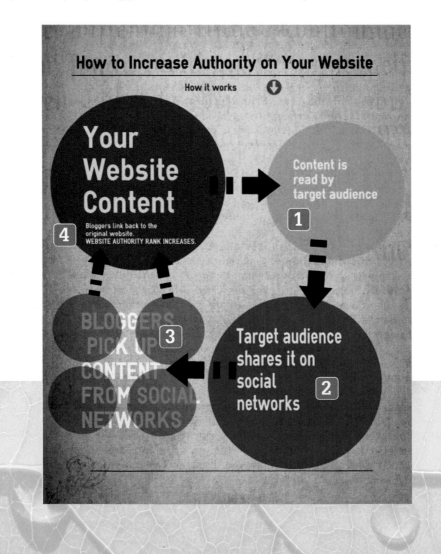

Thursday, 10 May 2012 01:32   Hits: 1486

2 Comments and 16 Reactions

Tweet 16   1   Digg↑   1   in Share 13   tumblr +

Buffer 3   Pin it   reddit this! 3   retweet   Like 7   +1 3

16
Tweet

1

13
in Share

tumblr

3
Buffer

0
Pin it

7
Like

3
+1

Capitalism, if it is to survive, has to change and social media is going to play a crucial role in the change, as well as the final form Capitalism will take.

We spend so much time of our working lives talking about the power of the team, team-building, leadership, empowerment, conceptualization, group dynamics and group performance that we forget, in all the psychobabble buzzwords and workshops just what a team does.

Teams have a simple function. They take people of different backgrounds and uneven abilities and normalize them in a way that enhances the team's performance. In this manner, the team becomes an entity that is much, much greater than the sum of its parts.

HOT TIP: Make your content easy to re-share by linking valuable tips and information to an entertaining, contemporary theme which is in the news or which is attracting a lot of attention.

DID YOU KNOW?
The authority of your website impacts directly upon its ranking and is decided by a complex combination of the number of sites linking back to you and the extent to which it is shared and re-shared.

HOT TIP: Include eye-catching, original images in your website content in order to increase the re-share value of your website content on social networks.

Use the real-time Web to increase your SEO

Learn to use the real-time Web to increase the search engine presence of your website by implementing all of the factors which go into making your website's content easy to share.

1 Increase your website's visibility in local search by including all localised information.

2 Have social sharing buttons on content and a link to your social media profiles where you can be followed.

3 Make sure your URLs are short and memorable.

4 Create content that people are more likely to respond to.

HOT TIP: Mobile search is playing an increasing role in the real-time Web. Even if you do not have a mobile website you should have set up your contact information with a real-world address and postcode and telephone numbers so you can take advantage of Google's local search results.

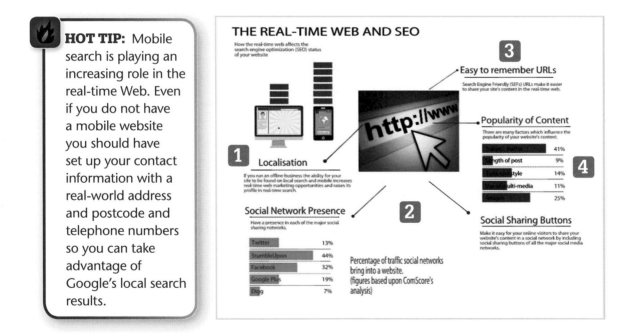

THE REAL-TIME WEB AND SEO

How the real-time web affects the search engine optimization (SEO) status of your website

3 Easy to remember URLs

Search Engine Friendly (SEFs) URLs make it easier to share your site's content in the real-time web.

Popularity of Content

There are many factors which influence the popularity of your website's content.

Subject matter	41%
Length of post	9%
Write style	14%
Use of multi-media	11%
Images	25%

4

1 Localisation

If you run an offline business the ability for your site to be found on local search and mobile increases real-time web marketing opportunities and raises its profile in real-time search.

Social Network Presence

Have a presence in each of the major social sharing networks.

Twitter	13%
StumbleUpon	44%
Facebook	32%
Google Plus	19%
Digg	7%

2 Percentage of traffic social networks bring into a website. (figures based upon ComScore's analysis)

Social Sharing Buttons

Make it easy for your online visitors to share your website's content in a social network by including social sharing buttons of all the major social media networks.

? DID YOU KNOW?

The real-time Web is produced mainly by the Twitter feed and Facebook's Wall stream, but is also informed by real-time sharing in other social networks with lower refresh rates.

HOT TIP: Use images which are closely related to your industry sector and what you do for maximum impact with your online visitors. Describe those images adequately to take advantage of Google's Image Search.

Use Twitter to increase your website's ranking

Use Twitter to take advantage of the presence of its data and significantly increase your website's SEO ranking.

1 Choose the content which you will share in Twitter.

2 Use hashtags '#' to mark the keywords under which this content should appear in Twitter search.

HOT TIP: Use the same keywords in Twitter, employing hashtags '#' as you would with the keywords on your website. Choose the best two or three keywords to help your website's content.

3 Use more than one keyword or category if your content permits it.

? DID YOU KNOW?
Use Twitter Search (https://twitter.com/#!/search-home) to determine how your content and website link rank in Twitter.

HOT TIP: When a Twitter profile makes the search results, search engines often use the bio as a description for the result. It needs to make sense and it needs to have relevant keywords. Always include city and postcode in your Twitter profile if you have a real-world business.

Use URL shorteners to increase your SEO

Use Bitly's URL shortening service (www.bitly.com) to increase the search engine indexing reach of your website and its content and help prepare it for semantic search.

1 Place the link you wish to shorten in the Bitly.com URL shortening field box.

2 Copy and use it anywhere.

3 Check out the statistics on URLs already shortened.

4 Look at the content you have already shared to gauge responses.

HOT TIP: Use Bitly.com as much as you can. The URL shortening service is building a search index of the data it captures and this can benefit your website hugely by providing an additional outlet for search.

WHAT DOES THIS MEAN?

Semantic search: A term applied to search which looks for the exact meaning of words as opposed to the match of one term with another which is what happens with conventional search.

DID YOU KNOW?

URL shorteners make it easier to re-share content on Twitter because they allow additional responses to be posted with the re-share, without exceeding the 140-character limit.

Save time in the real-time Web

Use Tweetdeck (www.tweetdeck.com) to monitor mentions in the real-time Web asynchronously, follow mentions of your name and posts, and engender interaction without having to wonder about time.

1 Create posts to appear in Twitter.

2 See mentions of your name.

3 Respond to anyone engaged with your content, all from one application.

HOT TIP: Use a web app like Buffer (www.buffer.com) to have your content Tweeted for you automatically at times when you are not online.

HOT TIP: Re-Tweet content which has already been re-Tweeted to refresh its reach and increase the number of people who will see it.

? DID YOU KNOW? Track Twitter posts through Tweetdeck as they are lost after about 90 minutes as the Twitter stream buries them, which means you miss the opportunities for interaction.

HOT TIP: Respond to every re-Tweet (RT) of your content by thanking the person who has re-Tweeted it. The engagement usually generates more interaction and leads to Twitter followers.

Top 10 Google Problems Solved

Problem 1: My website has dropped in search rankings

There are many reasons why a website may suddenly drop in search rankings. Check in your Google Webmaster Tools to see if there are any notifications.

1 See if there are any messages directly from Google.

2 Check to see if you have a large number of errors which may explain this.

3 Check to see how many of your URLs have been indexed.

HOT TIP: Google does not index all the URLs submitted even if you use a sitemap. As long as the number of pages indexed is greater than the number of pages not indexed, this is not something you need to worry about.

ALERT: Google updates its search algorithm practically every day. Do not panic if you notice a fluctuation in search rankings: it is normal when big changes happen. Monitor your website and see if it reverts to where it was in search within a day or two.

Problem 2: I am still not getting the traffic I used to get

Do a manual check of the Google Index to see how many pages of your website have been crawled and are in the Google Index.

 1 Go to Google.co.uk.

2 In the Search query box type site: http://mywebsitename.co.uk.

3 Check to see the number of pages which have been indexed.

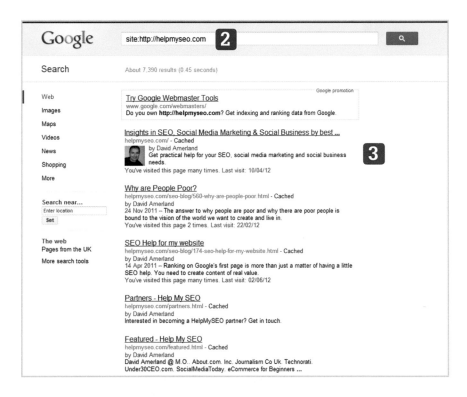

HOT TIP: Google handles the www and non-www versions of your website as separate websites unless you have taken the steps necessary in Webmaster Tools to tell it otherwise. Depending on which one you have set as your preference you will need to check that in the Google search box.

Problem 3: My images do not show up on Google Search

See whether your website images are indexed by Google by doing a check on Google Image Search using your website name.

1 Type the name of your website.

2 Check to see the images which come up first.

3 Check to see how many images come up from your website.

ALERT: Google cannot index images adequately if there are no description tags which detail what that image is.

4 Make sure that your website images had alt text entered when they were first placed on the site.

HOT TIP: You can improve the chances of your images appearing high on Google Image Search by making sure you use large, good-quality images in your website content.

Problem 4: My website traffic is dropping

Website traffic, like most things, can experience seasonal fluctuations. Use your Google Analytics account to check for seasonal peaks and troughs in your visitor numbers.

1 Go to Google Analytics.

2 Pick a period of at least 12 months to help you check your website's traffic stats.

3 Check to see where the peaks in traffic arise.

4 Check to see where the troughs in traffic are.

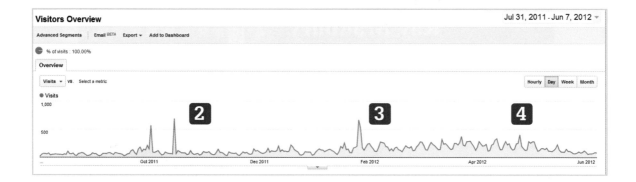

HOT TIP: There is a seasonality inherent in every business model. By identifying your website's traffic patterns you begin to get a sense of when dips in traffic are not a cause for real alarm.

Problem 5: My website traffic has still not recovered

Do not panic. If after a couple of weeks you see no improvement in your website traffic, you need to take action and go on the offensive.

1 Use every social media profile you have to promote your website's content in a sustained manner.

2 Use unique content suited to the audience in the social media in question.

3 Measure the effectiveness of what you are doing by getting social media metrics.

4 Point every social media effort back at your website and measure its effects by tracking visitor numbers.

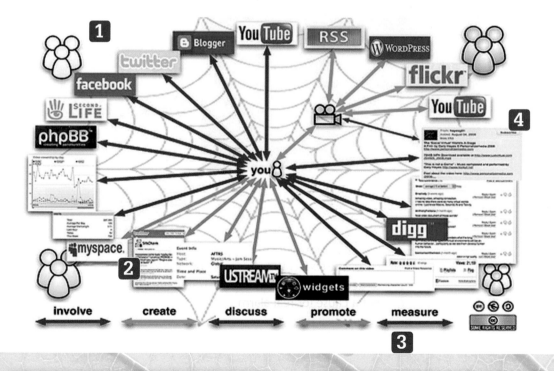

HOT TIP: Create a plan for how you will use the existing content on your website to attract social media attention. This will make it easier to coordinate your social media postings.

HOT TIP: Measure the effectiveness of each social media effort through Real-Time Google Analytics.

Problem 6: My website is not sticky enough

Stickiness is a problem for many websites. Online visitors have little time to stick around after reading the content they want.

1 Create content in a variety of formats.

2 Give your audience additional, popular and relevant content.

Problem 7: I cannot generate engagement in social media channels

The way social media success is measured is through interaction in comments, re-shares and responses.

1 Create content that is relevant and topical and share it in the right social network.

2 Compelling content always gets reactions.

3 Comments need to be responded to in order to continue to generate responses.

HOT TIP: Social media really is a conversation. Do not post content in social networks if you are not prepared to monitor it and respond to it.

ALERT: Keep your content relevant and interesting but shy away from controversial issues which touch upon race, politics or religion.

Problem 8: My keywords are not performing well

Identify specific keywords you can use by using data directly from Google. Go to http://goo.gl/C8c8g and use Google's Social Media Search to mine data directly.

1 Google Social Search is a customised search powered by Google's search technology.

2 Enter a search term directly related to what you do.

3 Click Search.

Google custom search

Social Media Search

2 [My Business Vertical] [Search] **3**

Search engine details

Inspired by a bittbox post*, this search engine searches only social bookmarking sites and specific blogs for the purpose of searching for freee downloadable things.

*

http://www.bittbox.com/rants/the-fastest-way-to-find-high-quality-freebies-on-the-web

searches sites including: hanleybrand.com, alistapart.com/, fontsquirrel.com/, thinkvitamin.com/, ajaxian.com/

Keywords: free stuff "social media" "web 2.0"

Last updated: January 29, 2011

Add this search engine to your Google homepage: [Google]
Add this search engine to your blog or webpage »

Create your own Custom Search Engine »

© 2012 Google - Google Home - About Google - Privacy Policy

HOT TIP: The search will reveal what is hot in social media in terms of content in your particular area. You can choose to copy (i.e. follow a trend) or buck the trend and create content that goes the other way. Use the results you uncover to help you target your content and keywords towards trending topics that help bring in traffic.

Problem 9: I do not know what content I need to create

Find out what people are searching for by using Google's Insights for search. It draws data directly from Google's Index and is an accurate tool when it comes to creating targeted content.

1 Go to the Real-Time Insights Finder at http://goo.gl/jymh3.

2 Click on What are people looking for?

3 Choose from the options available to get some helpful data.

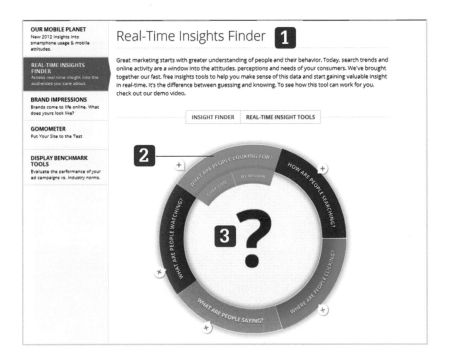

HOT TIP: Take the pressure off your content creation efforts by devising a 12-month content-creation plan which uses your research to produce an annual outline of what you need to create.

HOT TIP: Use any queries coming in through your website to help guide your content creation in a way that answers any questions your online visitors have.

Problem 10: How do I create a quality website?

Google is now judging website quality through its Panda and Penguin updates. Websites which are judged to be of higher quality rank higher in Google's search. Creating a website that Google sees as high quality is easy enough.

1 Use large, pictorial displays with no ads on the website.

2 Have multimedia content where possible.

3 Make good use of images.

4 Create original, topical content.

> 🔥 **HOT TIP:** Create content of different lengths to capture and hold the attention of people who have different attention spans and available reading time.

> 🔥 **HOT TIP:** Use headlines, pictures and multimedia files to break up the flow of bodies of text and help visitors navigate the content better.